# Three Israels

**Including**:

The Mystery of Black Israel

The Spiritual Roots of The Jewish People

The Spiritual Roots of
The Euro-Palestine - Israel Conflict

The Issue of Khazaria

For My Parents
Louis and Evelyn Goldstein

ISBN: 13: 978-0692272169
ISBN: 10: 069227216X

**Three Israels**
**Sheila R. Vitale**

# Living Epistles Ministries

Sheila R. Vitale
P O Box 562
Port Jefferson Station, NY 11776-0562 USA
(631) 331-1493

## Living Epistles Ministries

Sheila R. Vitale

Pastor, Teacher, Founder

PO Box 562

Port Jefferson Station, NY 11776 USA

# THREE ISRAELS

Including:

The Mystery of Black Israel

The Spiritual Roots of the Jewish People

The Spiritual Roots of the Euro-Palestine – Israel Conflict

The Issue of Khazaria

**Edited and Adapted as a Book by**
**Sheila R. Vitale**

## THREE ISRAELS

Is an Adaptation of a Transcript of **LEM Message #558, The Truth About Black Israel,** Which Was Transcribed and Edited For Clarity, Continuity of Thought, And Punctuation by

**The *LEM* Transcribing and Editing Team**

# Living Epistles Ministries
~ Judeo-Christian Spiritual Philosophy ~
## Sheila R. Vitale
### Pastor, Teacher & Founder

## Ministry Staff
Anthony Milton, Teacher (South Carolina)
Brooke Paige, Teacher (New York)
Sandra Aldrich (MN) (July 7, 1975 – April 18, 2021)

## Administrative Staff
Susan Panebianco, Office Manager

## Editorial Staff
Rose Herczeg, Editor

## Technical Staff
Lape Mobolaji-Lawal, Database Administrator

## Ministry Illustrators
Cecilia H. Bryant (Oct. 18, 1921 – Oct. 23, 2013)
Fidelis Onwubueke

## Music Staff
June Eble, Singer, Lyricist and Clarinetist
(July 20, 1931 – Jan. 24, 2024)
Don Gervais, Singer, Lyricist and Guitarist
Rita L. Rora, Singer, Lyricist and Guitarist

# Table of Contents

# The Alternate Translation Bible<sup>©</sup>

*The Alternate Translation Bible* **(ATB)** is an original translation of the Scripture.

Alternate Translation of the Old Testament<sup>©</sup>
Alternate Translation, Exodus, Chapter 32
    (Crime of the Calf)<sup>©</sup>
Alternate Translation, Daniel, Chapter 8<sup>©</sup>
Alternate Translation, Daniel, Chapter 11<sup>©</sup>

Alternate Translation of the New Testament<sup>©</sup>
Alternate Translation, 2 Thessalonians, Chapter 2
    (Sophia)<sup>©</sup>
Alternate Translation, 1<sup>st</sup> John, Chapter 5<sup>©</sup>
Alternate Translation, the Book of Colossians
    (To The Church At Colosse) <sup>©</sup>
Alternate Translation, the Book of Corinthians, Chapter 11
    (Corinthian Confusion) <sup>©</sup>
Alternate Translation, the Book of Jude
    (The Common Salvation)<sup>©</sup>

Alternate Translation of the Book of the Revelation of Jesus Christ
    to St. John<sup>©</sup>
Traducción Alternada del Libro de Revelación de Jesucristo<sup>©</sup>

For Additional Information, please contact:

# Alternate Translations in This Book

# Three Israels

**Including:**

The Mystery of Black Israel

The Spiritual Roots of The Jewish People

The Spiritual Roots of
The Euro-Palestine - Israel Conflict

The Issue of Khazaria

# I.

# ISRAEL

# I.

# ISRAEL

## Who or What Is Israel?

Israel is the nation that stands in front of Jehovah, the invisible God.

Jehovah first appeared from behind Nimrod, the son of Ham, and then, again, from behind Abraham and Jacob.

Nimrod was faithful to Jehovah. He ruled over Black Israel until he forgot that he was the personality that covered Jehovah, and thought that he, himself, was God.

> **Ezek 28:14,16** – *Covering Cherub*
>
> 14 THOU ART THE ANOINTED CHERUB THAT COVERETH; AND I HAVE SET THEE SO: THOU WAST UPON THE HOLY MOUNTAIN OF GOD; THOU HAST WALKED UP AND DOWN IN THE MIDST OF THE STONES OF FIRE.
>
> 16 BY THE MULTITUDE OF THY MERCHANDISE THEY HAVE FILLED THE MIDST OF THEE WITH VIOLENCE, **AND THOU HAST SINNED**: THEREFORE I WILL CAST THEE AS PROFANE OUT OF THE MOUNTAIN OF GOD: AND **I WILL DESTROY THEE, O COVERING CHERUB**, FROM THE MIDST OF THE STONES OF FIRE. **KJV**

After that Jehovah called Abraham . . .

### Gen 17:1 – *Abraham called*

> 17 AND WHEN ABRAM WAS NINETY YEARS OLD AND NINE, THE LORD APPEARED TO ABRAM, AND SAID UNTO HIM, I AM THE ALMIGHTY GOD; WALK BEFORE ME, AND BE THOU PERFECT. **KJV**

Nimrod was the sole ruler of Black Israel until Jehovah departed from him, but Jehovah appeared in many kings that descended from Abraham's family. Today, Jehovah is appearing through Jesus, and will be appearing in the near future, through Abraham's spiritual seed.

### Gal 3:16 – *Abraham's seed*

> 16 NOW TO ABRAHAM AND HIS SEED WERE THE PROMISES MADE. HE SAITH NOT, AND TO SEEDS, AS OF MANY; BUT AS OF ONE, **AND TO THY SEED, WHICH IS CHRIST. KJV**

At the end of the creation process, Israel will be one spiritual nation whose citizens come from every physical ethnicity. They will all share the same spiritual Blood and righteous nature of the Lord Jesus Christ.

### Acts 17:26 – *One Blood*

> 26 **AND HATH MADE OF ONE BLOOD ALL NATIONS OF MEN** FOR TO DWELL ON ALL THE FACE OF THE EARTH, AND HATH DETERMINED THE TIMES BEFORE APPOINTED, AND THE BOUNDS OF THEIR HABITATION; **KJV**

The in-gathering of the saints . . .

### Ex 23:16 – *Feast of Ingathering*

> 16 AND THE FEAST OF HARVEST, THE FIRSTFRUITS OF THY LABOURS, WHICH THOU HAST SOWN IN THE FIELD: AND **THE FEAST OF INGATHERING,** WHICH IS IN THE END OF THE YEAR, WHEN THOU HAST GATHERED IN THY LABOURS OUT OF THE FIELD. **KJV**

is the spiritual blending of physical Israel and the Israel of God, [1] the last Israel. Spiritual Israel will realize Jehovah's promises, which have been anticipated for generations.

> ### Gal 6:16 – *Israel of God*
>
> 16 AND AS MANY AS WALK ACCORDING TO THIS RULE, PEACE BE ON THEM, AND MERCY, AND UPON **THE ISRAEL OF GOD. KJV**

Jehovah's promises are fulfilled first in natural Israel and, after that, in Spiritual Israel . . .

> ### 1 Cor 15:46 – *Natural Then Spiritual*
>
> 46 HOWBEIT THAT WAS NOT **FIRST** WHICH IS SPIRITUAL, BUT **THAT WHICH IS NATURAL; AND AFTERWARD THAT WHICH IS SPIRITUAL. KJV**

# Nimrod

## *Spiritual Power through Wisdom*

Black Israel was rich in the spiritual power that is attained through wisdom. That same wisdom and power will appear again in Spiritual Israel, through the Christ Jesus.

# Abraham through Jacob

## *The Promise of Immortal Bodies*

Christ, Abraham's seed, provided an immortal body for Jesus, a descendant of Jacob and Judah, and will provide immortal bodies

---

[1] *The Israel of God*, also called **Spiritual Israel**, is Abraham's spiritual seed. This means that everyone who has **Abraham's nature** is Abraham's true descendant, and an heir to Jehovah's promises to Abraham.

for all of Jesus' spiritual offspring, the sons of God that comprise the Israel of God.

### Ex 32:13 – *Inheritance of Land*

13 REMEMBER ABRAHAM, ISAAC, AND ISRAEL, THY SERVANTS, TO WHOM THOU SWAREST BY THINE OWN SELF, AND SAIDST UNTO THEM, I WILL MULTIPLY YOUR SEED AS THE STARS OF HEAVEN, AND **ALL THIS LAND THAT I HAVE SPOKEN OF WILL I GIVE UNTO YOUR SEED, AND THEY SHALL INHERIT IT FOR EVER. KJV**

# Abraham & Jacob Through Moses

## *The Law*

Jehovah gave natural Israel the Law, through Moses, to help them to control their sinful tendencies . . .

### Ex 24:12 – *Ten Commandments*

12 AND THE LORD SAID UNTO MOSES, COME UP TO ME INTO THE MOUNT, AND BE THERE: AND **I WILL GIVE THEE TABLES OF STONE, AND A LAW, AND COMMANDMENTS** WHICH I HAVE WRITTEN; THAT THOU MAYEST TEACH THEM. **KJV**

and he is giving Spiritual Israel the power to live a sinless life through Christ Jesus.

### Heb 7:16 – *Endless Life*

16 WHO IS MADE, NOT AFTER THE LAW OF A CARNAL COMMANDMENT, BUT AFTER THE POWER OF **AN ENDLESS LIFE.** **KJV**

# Abraham & Jacob Through Joseph

### *The Mind Of God*

Hands signify the mind. Hands grasp material things and the mind grasps spiritual things.

Joseph's ability to interpret dreams and execute the office of viceroy over all of Pharaoh's kingdom, witnesses to the fact that Joseph had the mind of God.

> <u>Gen 49:24</u> – *Jacob Strengthened*
>
> 24 BUT HIS BOW ABODE IN STRENGTH, AND THE ARMS OF **HIS HANDS WERE MADE STRONG BY THE HANDS OF THE MIGHTY GOD OF JACOB**; (FROM THENCE IS THE SHEPHERD, THE STONE OF ISRAEL:) **KJV**

# Abraham & Jacob Through Judah

### *The Authority to Govern*

David and Solomon, the offspring of Judah, were kings of national Israel, and Jesus, Messiah, a descendant of Judah, is the king of spiritual Israel. Spiritual Israel is appearing in its individual citizens as of the publication of this book, but has not yet appeared publicly.

<u>Gen 49:10</u> – *Judah's Sceptre*

10 THE SCEPTRE SHALL NOT DEPART FROM JUDAH, NOR A LAWGIVER FROM BETWEEN HIS FEET, UNTIL SHILOH COME; AND UNTO HIM SHALL THE GATHERING OF THE PEOPLE BE. **KJV**

# Abraham, Jacob & Judah Through Jesus

## *The Righteous Seed*

National Israel had the righteousness of the Law, but Spiritual Israel has the true, internalized righteousness of Christ Jesus.

<u>Gen 49:24</u> – *Joseph, Stone of Israel*

24 BUT HIS BOW ABODE IN STRENGTH, AND THE ARMS OF HIS HANDS WERE MADE STRONG BY THE HANDS OF THE MIGHTY GOD OF JACOB; (FROM THENCE IS **THE SHEPHERD, THE STONE OF ISRAEL**:) **KJV**

<u>1 Cor 1:30</u> – *Christ Jesus Is Redemption*

30 BUT OF HIM ARE YE IN **CHRIST JESUS, WHO OF GOD IS MADE UNTO US WISDOM,** AND **RIGHTEOUSNESS,** AND **SANCTIFICATION,** AND **REDEMPTION: KJV**

# Abraham, Jacob, Judah Through the Man Christ Jesus

## *Eternal Life*

The glorified Jesus Christ is the Father of the Sons of God, a company of supernatural men, possessed by Christ Jesus, the only mediator between God and man.

### 1 Tim 2:5 – *One Mediator*

5 FOR THERE IS ONE GOD, AND **ONE MEDIATOR BETWEEN GOD AND MEN,** THE MAN CHRIST JESUS; **KJV**

# II.

# BLACK ISRAEL

# II.
# BLACK ISRAEL

## An Israel Before Israel

Several years ago a Black Christian wrote a book about how there was an African nation that served Jehovah before Abraham's Israel. He says that there was an Israel before the Israel of the Bible, who we know as *the chosen of God*. This pre-Israelite nation sinned, and they were cast down because of their idolatry and pride. After that, Jehovah offered His covenant to Abraham's Israel.

## Black Israel Today

The higher you are when you begin to descend, the lower you fall. We are presented, here, with a believable explanation as to why the African nations are still in such a desperate condition, even after the advent of Christianity. The spiritual world knows that Africa labors, even to this day, under heavy curses of idolatry and witchcraft, but we do not know the true reason why.

Why did Jehovah go to Abraham, a Shemite, before He went to a descendant of Ham? God always seeks to restore the most downtrodden and needy first, so why not Ham? We do not know if the curses afflicting Africa today were operating when Jehovah approached Shem. We know only that the progeny of Cush and

11

Nimrod are cursed because of their idolatry and rebellion against Jehovah.

Intellectually honest people will admit that sometimes there are still heavy curses on black people, even those who have the Holy Spirit. There is a black pastor in New York who is boldly preaching that.

The problems that black people face today are not the spiritual consequences of Noah's curse upon Canaan, because Africa descends from Cush and Nimrod, not from Canaan. So, the curses that black people face today, appear to be the fruit of the idolatry that Nimrod and his followers fell into while they were serving as Jehovah's mediator nation.

Africa, Black Israel, is experiencing Jehovah's righteous Sowing & Reaping Judgment, right up to this very day.

Idolatry is still practiced across the continent of Africa today. The land is cursed, and that curse has not been lifted by the Holy Spirit. That curse can only be lifted by Christ Jesus, as he comes forth within the African people and Black people everywhere.

### Christ Jesus Will Deliver Africa

There are a lot of Holy Spirit Christians in Africa today who still have a strong spirit of witchcraft. Some go to Holy Ghost churches, but still have witchcraft so deeply ingrained within them that they cannot tell the difference between the Holy Spirit and a spirit of witchcraft.

**2 Cor 11:14** – *Satan Transformed*

> 14 AND NO MARVEL; FOR **SATAN HIMSELF IS TRANSFORMED INTO AN ANGEL OF LIGHT. KJV**

It will take Christ Jesus appearing in the individual to swallow up that witchcraft and break the curses on the individual first, and then on Africa, at large. Africa is waiting for Christ Jesus.

# Nimrod & Black Israel

### *Good Before He Was Bad*

Nimrod headed up Black Israel, the first nation in the earth to worship one God. Nimrod and his followers served Jehovah faithfully until they turned to idolatrous pagan practices. After that, they became Jehovah's enemies, and he cast them down. Nimrod's lust for power eventually overtook him, and he became a tyrant and the enemy of the people that he was sent to save.

### *Ham and Noah*

Ham, Nimrod's ancestor, is the only one of Noah's three sons who recognized that Noah had been seduced by the intoxicating personality of the emotional waters of Sheol. Noah's sin severed the connection between Noah and Primordial Adam, and ended Noah's ministry as the only mediator between God and mankind at that time.[2]

Noah's soul had been resident in Shem, Ham and Japheth in the form of Righteous Adam, their higher mind, so when Noah's attachment to Primordial Adam was severed, Righteous Adam within Shem and Japheth dissolved.

---

[2] See, *the Noah Chronicles*, CCK Message #816.

Noah's failure sold Shem and Japheth into spiritual slavery, and their souls were trapped under the mind of fallen Adam within mortal mankind, the earthen creature that they were sent to save.

After that, Ham inherited Noah's office, and two generations later, Ham incarnated in the earth through his grandson, Nimrod.

Nimrod's assignment was to establish a mediator nation in the earth which would teach the rest of humanity about Jehovah, the one true God.

But, tragedy struck, once again. Ham sinned, and like Noah before him, Ham's connection to Primordial Adam was severed.

But Nimrod's fate was much worse than that of Shem and Japheth. Nimrod became an evil tyrant, and completely corrupted the purpose for his incarnation, which was to be a savior to mankind.

Nimrod made himself the object of worship and tyrannized the people, wherefore, the Scripture says:

> **Gen 10:9 - AT: Nimrod, The Tyrant.** *Nimrod, the personality that revealed Jehovah's nature, became a powerful tyrant who consumed the life force of God's people.* **(ATB)**

Nimrod misused Jehovah's power, and some say that it was Abraham, Jehovah's hand-picked replacement, that executed Nimrod to reclaim Jehovah's spiritual authority. After that, Abraham replaced Nimrod's Israel through the progeny of his sons, Isaac, Jacob, Joseph and, finally, Ephraim, the firstborn of the fused DNA of Nimrod and Abraham.[3]

---

[3] See, Ephraim, and Manassah, p 23

### *Holy DNA*

Africa is still experiencing Jehovah's righteous judgment for turning to idolatry when they knew the Most High God, but a remnant of Nimrodian Israel preserved the spiritual knowledge that Noah brought from the other side of the Flood, and re-emerged to found Egypt, the land of spiritual mysteries.

After that, Jehovah joined the faithful remnant of repentant Nimrodians scattered throughout Egypt to a small, insignificant tribe of shepherds, the descendants of Abraham, Jehovah's friend . . .

> **James 2:23** – *Abraham, God's Friend*
>
> 23 AND THE SCRIPTURE WAS FULFILLED WHICH SAITH, **ABRAHAM BELIEVED GOD**, AND IT WAS IMPUTED UNTO HIM FOR RIGHTEOUSNESS: **AND HE WAS CALLED THE FRIEND OF GOD. KJV**

and planted the seeds of the Ham's preserved knowledge, wisdom and spiritual power in Israel, Jehovah's **Firstborn Son**, the offspring of the blended DNA of Nimrod and Abraham, Jacob and Joseph.

# III.

# ABRAHAM'S ISRAEL

# III.
# ABRAHAM'S ISRAEL

## Jacob

Jehovah told Abraham that his descendants would be enslaved in Egypt for a season, and then leave there with great spiritual riches. . . .

> **Gen 15:13** – *Strangers in a Land*
>
> 13 AND HE SAID UNTO ABRAM, KNOW OF A SURETY THAT **THY SEED SHALL BE A STRANGER IN A LAND THAT IS NOT THEIRS, AND SHALL SERVE THEM; AND THEY SHALL AFFLICT THEM FOUR HUNDRED YEARS**; **KJV**

Oh, you thought Jehovah meant gold, money and jewels? Really?

I always wondered, why Jehovah would actually plan the enslavement of Abraham's descendants. Today I understand that Jehovah did not *desire* Jacob's enslavement, but He did *require* the *fusion* of the seed of Jacob, the second Patriarch of Abraham's Israel, with the physical royalty and spiritual riches of Egypt, the guardian of the mysteries of antiquity.

Did you ever wonder why Jacob made Ephraim and Manasseh equal to Joseph's brothers, their uncles? . . .

### Gen 48:5 – *Ephraim and Manasseh*

> 5 AND NOW THY TWO SONS, **EPHRAIM AND MANASSEH,** WHICH WERE BORN UNTO THEE IN THE LAND OF EGYPT BEFORE I CAME UNTO THEE INTO EGYPT, **ARE MINE; AS REUBEN AND SIMEON, THEY SHALL BE MINE. KJV**

Did you ever wonder why or how Ephraim became so important that he represents the collective ten tribes of Israel?

### Jer 31:20 – *Ephraim, God's Son*

> 20 IS **EPHRAIM MY DEAR SON**? IS HE A PLEASANT CHILD? FOR SINCE I SPAKE AGAINST HIM, I DO EARNESTLY REMEMBER HIM STILL: THEREFORE MY BOWELS ARE TROUBLED FOR HIM; I WILL SURELY HAVE MERCY UPON HIM, SAITH THE LORD. **KJV**

Ephraim and Manasseh are the spiritual and genetic fusion of

*Jacob, the shepherd*, through Joseph, their father, and the spiritual and genetic greatness of

*Seth, Nimrod and Egypt*, through Asenath, the daughter of Poti-pherah, priest of On. . . .

### Gen 41:45 – *Joseph's Wife*

> 45 AND PHARAOH CALLED JOSEPH'S NAME ZAPHNATH-PAANEAH; AND **HE GAVE HIM TO WIFE ASENATH THE DAUGHTER OF POTI-PHERAH PRIEST OF ON.** AND JOSEPH WENT OUT OVER ALL THE LAND OF EGYPT. **KJV**

Surely, Ephraim and Manasseh were as instructed in the wisdom of Egypt, as was Moses, who grew up in Pharaoh's house. If we would dare to think in terms of science fiction, we might even say that Jacob (and his descendants, of course) were the new bodies that the spiritual and genetic greatness of Nimrod were to be joined to.

***Ephraim***, the elder of the two tribes with the fused DNA of Nimrod and Abraham, Jacob and Joseph, inherited the office of the ***Firstborn of Israel*** with the right of primogeniture . . .

### Gen 48:18-19 – *Ephraim Greater*

18 AND JOSEPH SAID UNTO HIS FATHER, NOT SO, MY FATHER: FOR THIS IS THE FIRSTBORN; PUT THY RIGHT HAND UPON HIS HEAD.

19 AND HIS FATHER REFUSED, AND SAID, I KNOW IT, MY SON, I KNOW IT: HE ALSO SHALL BECOME A PEOPLE, AND HE ALSO SHALL BE GREAT: BUT TRULY **HIS YOUNGER BROTHER SHALL BE GREATER THAN HE**, AND HIS SEED SHALL BECOME A MULTITUDE OF NATIONS. **KJV**

and became the primary tribe of the Northern Kingdom of Abraham's Israel. Remember that Joseph inherited the right of Jacob's firstborn . . .

### Gen 37:9 – *Joseph's Dreams*

9 AND HE DREAMED YET ANOTHER DREAM, AND TOLD IT HIS BRETHREN, AND SAID, BEHOLD, I HAVE DREAMED A DREAM MORE; AND, BEHOLD, **THE SUN AND THE MOON AND THE ELEVEN STARS MADE OBEISANCE TO ME.** **KJV**

after Reuben, Levi and Simeon were rejected. Judah was next in line, but one tribe could not bring forth both aspects of Messiah: The Lawgiver, through a royal line of kings, . . .

### Gen 49:10 – *Judah's Septre*

10 **THE SCEPTRE SHALL NOT DEPART FROM JUDAH,** NOR A LAWGIVER FROM BETWEEN HIS FEET, UNTIL SHILOH COME; AND UNTO HIM SHALL THE GATHERING OF THE PEOPLE BE. **KJV**

and the righteous seed. Messiah's two offices, one from the tribe of Judah and the other from the tribe of Ephraim, will be joined in the third Israel, ***the Israel of God***.

# Moses

Abraham's Israel received

The promise of immortal bodies, Messiah and royalty through Judah . . .

### Gen 49:10 - *Judah's Sceptre*

10 THE SCEPTRE SHALL NOT DEPART FROM JUDAH, NOR A LAWGIVER FROM BETWEEN HIS FEET, UNTIL SHILOH COME; AND UNTO HIM SHALL THE GATHERING OF THE PEOPLE BE.  **KJV**

The seed of a righteous nature through Joseph . . .

### Gen 49:24 – *The Stone of Israel*

24 BUT HIS BOW ABODE IN STRENGTH, AND THE ARMS OF HIS HANDS WERE MADE STRONG BY THE HANDS OF THE MIGHTY GOD OF JACOB; (*FROM THENCE IS THE SHEPHERD, THE STONE OF ISRAEL*:)  **KJV**

and

Seth's genetic and spiritual greatness which was buried in the Egyptian descendants of Nimrodian Israel.

### Gen 4:25 - *Seth*

25 AND ADAM KNEW HIS WIFE AGAIN; AND SHE BARE A SON, AND CALLED HIS NAME SETH: FOR **GOD, SAID SHE, HATH APPOINTED ME ANOTHER SEED** INSTEAD OF ABEL, WHOM CAIN SLEW. **KJV**

Jehovah fused the DNA of the two nations through Joseph's marriage to Asenath, and called that dual seed, ***Israel, His Firstborn Son.***

Jehovah knew that the shepherds of Abraham's Israel were simple men, and that the fusion of Abraham's Israel with the spiritual power and wisdom of fallen Black Israel, would eventually overwhelm them.

Joseph carried the righteous seed, and was not corrupted by Egyptian idolatry and witchcraft, and Jacob served Jehovah faithfully to his death. But Ephraim and Manasseh inherited Nimrod's fallen blood, as well as the blood of faithful Abraham, and did not rise to the greatness of Abraham and Jacob, the two patriarchs who were their fathers.

# Ephraim and Manasseh

Ephraim and Manasseh, like Christian Israel today, struggled with their two natures . . .

<u>James 1:8</u> – *Double minded Man*

> 8 A **DOUBLE MINDED MAN** IS UNSTABLE IN ALL HIS WAYS. **KJV**

but failed to take the victory, and Abraham's Israel fell into idolatry under their leadership. The fused DNA of Seth through Nimrod, and Jacob through Joseph, and the royal DNA of Judah that Jehovah called *His Son, Israel*, was trapped in the physical bodies of Abraham's Israel, just like Seth's spiritual and genetic greatness was trapped in the physical bodies of the Egyptians. So, Jehovah sent Moses, a savior who would distinguish between the people of Abraham's Israel who were seeded with *Jehovah's Firstborn Son,* and those who were not.

### Two Grades of Wisdom

***Pharaoh*** and ***the king of Egypt*** signify two grades of unrighteous spiritual wisdom that dominated ***Israel, Jehovah's Firstborn Son,*** from within. Moses, as Jehovah's agent, taught the people how to rule over the King of Egypt, their lower, unrighteous side, . . .

**Ex 4:3** – *Moses' Rod*

3 AND HE SAID, CAST IT ON THE GROUND. AND **HE CAST IT ON THE GROUND, AND IT BECAME A SERPENT;** AND MOSES FLED FROM BEFORE IT. **KJV**

by understanding their dual nature . . .

**James 4:8** – *Double minded*

8 DRAW NIGH TO GOD, AND HE WILL DRAW NIGH TO YOU. CLEANSE YOUR HANDS, YE SINNERS; AND PURIFY YOUR HEARTS, **YE DOUBLE MINDED. KJV**

and a knowledge of the Law.

**Ex 20:1-3** – *No Other Gods*

1 AND GOD SPAKE ALL THESE WORDS, SAYING,

2 I AM THE LORD THY GOD, WHICH HAVE BROUGHT THEE OUT OF THE LAND OF EGYPT, OUT OF THE HOUSE OF BONDAGE.

3 **THOU SHALT HAVE NO OTHER GODS BEFORE ME.** **KJV**

# Moses & the Ethiopian Woman

Some say that Miriam and Aaron opposed Moses' remarriage because they were jealous of his sexual or romantic involvement with this enigmatic Ethiopian woman.

### Num 12:1 – *Ethiopian Woman*

> 1 AND MIRIAM AND AARON SPAKE AGAINST MOSES BECAUSE OF THE **ETHIOPIAN WOMAN** WHOM HE HAD MARRIED: FOR HE HAD MARRIED AN ETHIOPIAN WOMAN. **KJV**

Others say that Zipporah was the Ethiopian woman. Yet others say that Miriam and Aaron were prejudiced against Moses' black wife.

## *Miriam's Sin*

Jehovah told Moses that Joshua was to succeed him and Moses told Miriam and Aaron, but Miriam didn't take the news very well. Miriam thought that she and Aaron, Moses' blood siblings, or at least a Levite or immediate relative, should inherit his office, especially Aaron, who went with Moses to challenge Pharaoh.

Miriam could not understand why Moses would choose Joshua instead of a blood relative.

Miriam sinned against Moses when she challenged his authority, saying, *Aaron and I hear from God as well as you, Moses. Why would you choose a successor from another family*?

### Num 12:2 – *Miriam's Envy*

> 2 AND THEY SAID, **HATH THE LORD INDEED SPOKEN ONLY BY MOSES**? HATH HE NOT SPOKEN ALSO BY US? AND THE LORD HEARD IT. **KJV**

But the more serious sin, the sin that produced the judgment of Leprosy . . .

### Num 12:10 – *Miriam Leprous*

> 10 AND THE CLOUD DEPARTED FROM OFF THE TABERNACLE; AND, BEHOLD, MIRIAM BECAME LEPROUS, WHITE AS SNOW: AND AARON LOOKED UPON MIRIAM, **AND, BEHOLD, SHE WAS LEPROUS. KJV**

was Miriam's judgment that Moses, the man, rather than Jehovah, chose Joshua. Miriam did not recognize the Spirit of Jehovah speaking through Moses because her own desires overshadowed the mind of the prophetess within her.

### Ex 15:20 – *Miriam the Prophetess*

> 20 AND **MIRIAM THE PROPHETESS,** THE SISTER OF
> AARON, TOOK A TIMBREL IN HER HAND; AND ALL THE WOMEN
> WENT OUT AFTER HER WITH TIMBRELS AND WITH DANCES.
> KJV

Miriam's first sin was criticizing Jehovah, and her second sin was imputing an ungodly motive to Moses, the man of God.

### 1 Chron 23:14 – *Moses, Man of God*

> 14 NOW CONCERNING **MOSES THE MAN OF GOD,** HIS
> SONS WERE NAMED OF THE TRIBE OF LEVI. **KJV**

It is a very serious sin to impute a wrong motive to a man of God, because doing so calls the Spirit of God that speaks through him unclean.

### *Aaron's Sin*

Aaron might have desired Moses' office for himself, but it is unlikely that he denied that Jehovah, and not Moses, had chosen Joshua.

Nevertheless, Aaron failed to stop Miriam from denying Jehovah's Spirit. He also failed to stop her from saying that Moses, himself, chose Joshua, thus imputing an ungodly motive to the mortal man, Moses. Aaron was, then, in this way, complicit, in Miriam's wrong doing.

Wherefore, Heaven includes Aaron in its indictment, saying . . . *And Miriam and Aaron spake against Moses because . . . he had*

***married an Ethiopian woman . . . saying, Hath the Lord, indeed, spoken only by Moses? Hath he not spoken also by us?***

### Num 12:1-2 –*Aaron's Sin*

1 AND **MIRIAM AND AARON SPAKE AGAINST MOSES** BECAUSE OF THE ETHIOPIAN WOMAN WHOM HE HAD MARRIED: FOR HE HAD MARRIED AN ETHIOPIAN WOMAN.

2 AND THEY SAID, **HATH THE LORD INDEED SPOKEN ONLY BY MOSES**? HATH HE NOT SPOKEN ALSO BY US? AND THE LORD HEARD IT. **KJV**

Aaron repented of his sin . . .

### Num 12:11 – *Aaron Repents*

11 AND **AARON SAID** UNTO MOSES, ALAS, MY LORD, **I BESEECH THEE, LAY NOT THE SIN UPON US**, WHEREIN WE HAVE DONE FOOLISHLY, AND WHEREIN WE HAVE SINNED. **KJV**

and then interceded for Miriam.

### Num 12:12 – *Miriam Leprous*

12 LET **HER NOT BE AS ONE DEAD**, OF WHOM THE FLESH IS HALF CONSUMED WHEN HE COMETH OUT OF HIS MOTHER'S WOMB. **KJV**

Moses forgave Aaron, and accepted Aaron's petition for mercy for Miriam . . .

### Num 12:13 – *Moses Intercedes*

13 AND MOSES CRIED UNTO THE LORD, SAYING, **HEAL HER NOW, O GOD, I BESEECH THEE. KJV**

but there is no record of Miriam repenting or asking for mercy. One might wonder if Miriam's leprosy might have been avoided, or the time that she spent outside of the Israelite camp shortened, had Miriam repented.

It is interesting to note the similarity between Aaron's apparent inability to prevent Miriam from denigrating Moses' motive for choosing Joshua, and his inability to prevent the Hebrew children from making a golden calf.

### *Joshua, the Ethiopian Woman*

Why would the Scripture speak about an ***Ethiopian woman***, and not name her?

A physical man can be a spiritual woman, so maybe this Ethiopian woman was a physical man.

Moses never re-married, but, rather, ascended to a high spiritual place where there is no physical marriage.

> <u>**Matt 22:30**</u> *– No Marriage In Heaven*
>
> 30 FOR IN THE RESURRECTION **THEY NEITHER MARRY, NOR ARE GIVEN IN MARRIAGE,** BUT ARE AS THE ANGELS OF GOD IN HEAVEN. **KJV**

Joshua and Moses shared a teacher-disciple intimacy that can be defined as a spiritual marriage, so Joshua could have been the Ethiopian woman.

Now, Joshua would surely have been a spiritual female in relation to Moses, but was Joshua an Ethiopian?

The designation ***Ethiopian*** describes any descendant of Cush,[4] one of the sons of Ham, so Moses' Ethiopian woman had to be a descendant of Cush, but not necessarily an Ethiopian.

Egypt is in Africa, and its inhabitants are descendants of Ham, the father of Cush. . . .

> ### Gen 10:6 – *Joshua, An Ephrathite*
>
> 6 AND **JOSHUA, SONS OF HAM; CUSH**, AND MIZRAIM, AND PHUT, AND CANAAN. **KJV**

Joshua was an Ephriamite, . . .

> ### Num 13:8 – *Son of Nun*
>
> 8 OF THE TRIBE OF EPHRAIM, **OSHEA THE SON OF NUN. KJV**

from the tribe of Ephraim, the offspring of Joseph and Asenath Joseph's Egyptian wife. So Joshua was an Egyptian and a Cushite.

Joshua's relationship to Moses was similar to John's relationship to Jesus . . .

> ### John 13:25 – *Jesus' Favorite*
>
> 25 HE THEN **LYING ON JESUS' BREAST** SAITH UNTO HIM, LORD, WHO IS IT? **KJV**

Jehovah told Moses to prepare Joshua to lead the Israelite armies after he died, which preparation requires the close soul tie of teacher and disciple, sometimes called a ***spiritual marriage***.

---

[4] Unger's Bible Dictionary.

Joshua was Moses' disciple. The two were very close -- they were spiritually intimate.

Joshua is the Ethiopian woman.

# Moses and Zipporah

Jehovah chose Moses to liberate the Hebrew children, but Zipporah, Moses' Midianite wife, was not about to let him go.

### *The Matter of Peor*

Zipporah was a high priestess[5] of Baal-Peor . . .

**Num 25:18 –** *Matter of Peor*

> **18** FOR THEY VEX YOU WITH THEIR WILES, WHEREWITH **THEY HAVE BEGUILED YOU IN THE MATTER OF PEOR, KJV**

where the Midianite women seduced the Israelite men to worship Ba'al Peor . . .

**Num 25:2 –** *Other gods*

> **2 AND THEY CALLED THE PEOPLE UNTO THE SACRIFICES OF THEIR GODS**: AND THE PEOPLE DID EAT, AND BOWED DOWN TO THEIR GODS. **KJV**

---

[5] The name *Zipporah*, means *little female bird*, and the name, *Zippor*, in *Balak, son of* **Zippor**, means **little male bird.**

*Balak, King of Moab*, was a black magician who tried to hire Balaam, the sorcerer, to help him curse Israel.

and Zipporah was an ancestor of the infamous Cozbi, one of the Midianitish woman who were seducing the Israelite men to worship Baal-Peor . . .

### Num 25:15 & 18 - *Cozbi*

15 AND THE NAME OF THE MIDIANITISH WOMAN THAT WAS SLAIN WAS COZBI, THE DAUGHTER OF ZUR; HE WAS HEAD OVER A PEOPLE, AND OF A CHIEF HOUSE IN MIDIAN.

18. . . AND IN THE MATTER OF COZBI, THE DAUGHTER OF A PRINCE OF MIDIAN, THEIR SISTER WHICH WAS SLAIN IN THE DAY OF THE PLAGUE FOR PEOR'S SAKE. KJV

and Zimri , a Simeonite prince . . .

### Num 25:14 – *Zimri's Adultery*

14 NOW THE NAME OF THE ISRAELITE THAT WAS SLAIN, EVEN THAT WAS SLAIN WITH THE MIDIANITISH WOMAN, WAS ZIMRI, THE SON OF SALU, A PRINCE OF A CHIEF HOUSE AMONG THE SIMEONITES. KJV

brought Cozbi, who was Midianite royalty, the daughter of a prince, into the Israelite camp . . .

### Num 25:6 – *Midianitish Woman*

6 AND, BEHOLD, ONE OF THE CHILDREN OF ISRAEL CAME AND BROUGHT UNTO HIS BRETHREN A MIDIANITISH WOMAN IN THE SIGHT OF MOSES . . . KJV

where many Israelites were dying from the plague that Jehovah was plaguing Israel with, because they were worshipping Ba'al Peor . . .

### Num 25:6 – *Weeping For Tammuz*

> 6 . . . AND IN THE SIGHT OF ALL THE CONGREGATION OF **THE CHILDREN OF ISRAEL, WHO WERE WEEPING BEFORE THE DOOR OF THE TABERNACLE OF THE CONGREGATION.** **KJV**

and Phineas, the grandson of Aaron, slew both Zimri and Cozbi as they fornicated openly before all Israel.

### Num 25:7 – *Phinehas, the, Hero*

> 7 AND WHEN **PHINEHAS, THE SON OF ELEAZAR, THE SON OF AARON THE PRIEST, SAW IT,** HE ROSE UP FROM AMONG THE CONGREGATION, AND TOOK A JAVELIN IN HIS HAND; **KJV**

Phinehas, Aaron's grandson, executed Cozbi and Zimri, her lover, a Simeonite prince . . .

### Num 25:8 – *Cozbi and Zimri Slain*

> 8 AND HE WENT AFTER THE MAN OF ISRAEL INTO THE TENT, AND **THRUST BOTH OF THEM THROUGH,** THE MAN OF ISRAEL, AND THE WOMAN THROUGH HER BELLY . . . **KJV**

and stopped the plague that had already killed twenty-four thousand.

### Num 25:9,8,4 – *24,000 Dead At Peor*

> 9 AND THOSE THAT DIED IN THE PLAGUE WERE **TWENTY AND FOUR THOUSAND,** AND
>
> 8. . . . SO THE PLAGUE WAS STAYED FROM THE CHILDREN OF ISRAEL.

> **4** AND THE LORD SAID UNTO MOSES, **TAKE ALL
> THE HEADS OF THE PEOPLE,** AND HANG THEM UP BEFORE THE
> LORD AGAINST THE SUN, **THAT THE FIERCE ANGER OF THE
> LORD** MAY BE TURNED AWAY FROM **ISRAEL. KJV**

Zipporah was of the same generation of Midianitish women that seduced Israel, a nation defended by Jehovah. Zipporah's witchcraft was so powerful that it would have turned Moses, the man of God, away from Jehovah, were it not for Jehovah's direct intervention on Moses' behalf. [6]

Jehovah rescued the nation of Israel in the matter of Peor at the cost of many Israelite lives, but he saved one man, Moses, by a direct challenge to the sorceress that was possessing his mind, will and emotions.

Moses was on God's side at Peor, but he appears to have been captured by Zipporah's witchcraft during his early years of separation.

### *Moses, From Egypt to Midian*

Moses was fully immersed in Egyptian society and the mysteries of Egyptian religion, when a Hebrew man, acting out of the nature of Pharaoh, threatened him

#### Ex 2:14 – *Moses Afraid*

> 14 AND HE SAID, WHO MADE THEE A PRINCE AND A
> JUDGE OVER US? INTENDEST THOU TO KILL ME, AS THOU
> KILLEDST THE EGYPTIAN? **AND MOSES FEARED,** AND SAID,
> SURELY THIS THING IS KNOWN. **KJV**

Moses left Egypt after that . . .

---

[6] See, *Moses' Spiritual Circumcision*, p 49

### Ex 2:15 – *Moses Flees*

> 15 NOW WHEN PHARAOH HEARD THIS THING, HE
> SOUGHT TO SLAY MOSES. BUT **MOSES FLED FROM THE FACE**
> **OF PHARAOH,** AND DWELT IN THE LAND OF MIDIAN: AND HE
> SAT DOWN BY A WELL. **KJV**

but not because Jehovah told him to go. Moses left Egypt because he was afraid of the people that Jehovah sent him to rescue.

At this point in time, Jacob's descendants had been in Egypt for 300 years, and were most likely fully integrated into Egyptian culture.

It is interesting to note that Moses fled from *the face of* Pharaoh. The Hebrew word translated *face* is frequently translated *personality*, indicating that Moses fled from a Hebrew man who had the personality of Pharaoh.

In other words, Moses did not flee from Pharaoh, the king of Egypt. Moses fled from a Hebrew man that was so assimilated into Egyptian culture, that for all intents and purposes, he was an Egyptian.

The same Moses that fled from the Hebrew-Egyptian man, fled from Jehovah, as well, and returned to pagan worship as a part of the new life that he built for himself with Zipporah, his wife.

Moses probably thought that Jehovah would never come looking for him and, desiring peace with his wife, agreed as much as possible with Zipporah.

### *Moses, The Married Man*

Moses and Zipporah, the married couple, with their two sons, Gershom and Eliezer, were a family, a single spiritual, emotional and mental unit. Moses and Zipporah were one flesh, . . .

#### <u>Gen 2:24</u> – *One Flesh*

> 24 THEREFORE SHALL A MAN LEAVE HIS FATHER AND HIS MOTHER, AND SHALL CLEAVE UNTO HIS WIFE: **AND THEY SHALL BE ONE FLESH.** KJV

one soul, and neither of them ever expected to be separated for any reason other than death.

But, then, suddenly, without any warning, God called to Moses out of a burning bush.

#### <u>Ex 3:2</u> – *Burning Bush*

> 2 AND **THE ANGEL OF THE LORD** APPEARED UNTO **HIM IN A FLAME OF FIRE OUT OF THE MIDST OF A BUSH:** AND HE LOOKED, AND, BEHOLD, THE BUSH BURNED WITH FIRE, AND THE BUSH WAS NOT CONSUMED. **KJV**

and Jehovah said . . .

**Ex 4:21 - AT:  Moses Returns to Egypt.** *Moses, go and return to Egypt, and [let the people] see all the miraculous signs that I have put in your mind to do, but Pharaoh will seize the hearts of the people and not let them go* **(ATB)**

Moses, the man of God, responded to the call, and asked his father-in-law, Jethro, who was also his employer, for permission to go . . .

### Ex 4:18 – *Jethro Releases Moses*

> 18 AND MOSES WENT AND RETURNED TO JETHRO HIS FATHER IN LAW, AND SAID UNTO HIM, **LET ME GO, I PRAY THEE, AND RETURN UNTO MY BRETHREN WHICH ARE IN EGYPT**, AND SEE WHETHER THEY BE YET ALIVE. AND JETHRO SAID TO MOSES, GO IN PEACE. **KJV**

packed up his family and left for Egypt, where he was to assume the leadership of the Hebrew people.

### Ex 4:20 – *Moses & Zipporah To Egypt*

> 20 AND **MOSES TOOK HIS WIFE AND HIS SONS,** AND SET THEM UPON AN ASS, AND HE RETURNED TO THE LAND OF EGYPT: AND MOSES TOOK THE ROD OF GOD IN HIS HAND. **KJV**

Well, what a shock it must have been for Moses and Zipporah when Jehovah encountered them as they began their journey, and threatened to kill their son!

### Ex 4:24 – *Jehovah Encounters Moses*

> 24 AND IT CAME TO PASS BY THE WAY IN THE INN, THAT **THE LORD MET HIM, AND SOUGHT TO KILL HIM** **KJV**

# Jehovah and Zipporah

Now, we can stay with the letter of the Word and believe that Jehovah is such a vengeful God that he would have killed Moses for not circumcising the boy, or killed the boy, as some believe, or we can look for the spiritual understanding of the Scripture.

Jehovah makes it very clear throughout the Scripture that He is *The God*, the ruler of heaven and earth, and that He owns everything therein. He owns all the cattle, . . .

### Ps 50:10 – *God Owns Everything*

10 FOR EVERY BEAST OF THE FOREST IS MINE, AND
THE CATTLE UPON A THOUSAND HILLS. **KJV**

and all the property. He can take the land of Canaan away from the
Canaanites and give it to the Israelites if He chooses to do so, and
no one can stop him.

Who, then, would resist Jehovah when He takes their husband,
wife, or son? , . . .

### 1 Sam 1:28 – *Lent to the Lord*

28 THEREFORE ALSO **I HAVE LENT HIM TO THE
LORD; AS LONG AS HE LIVETH HE SHALL BE LENT TO THE
LORD.** AND HE WORSHIPPED THE LORD THERE. **KJV**

or daughter? . . .

### Judge 11:39 – *Jethro's Daughter*

39 AND IT CAME TO PASS AT THE END OF TWO
MONTHS THAT SHE RETURNED UNTO HER FATHER, WHO DID
WITH HER ACCORDING TO HIS VOW WHICH HE HAD VOWED:
**AND SHE KNEW NO MAN.** AND IT WAS A CUSTOM IN ISRAEL.
**KJV**

Even, Elisha . . .

### 1 Kings 19:20-21 – *Elisha Follows Elijah*

20 AND HE LEFT THE OXEN, AND RAN AFTER ELIJAH,
AND SAID, **LET ME, I PRAY THEE, KISS MY FATHER AND MY
MOTHER, AND THEN I WILL FOLLOW THEE.** AND HE SAID
UNTO HIM, GO BACK AGAIN: FOR WHAT HAVE I DONE TO THEE?

21 THEN HE AROSE, AND WENT AFTER ELIJAH, AND
MINISTERED UNTO HIM. **KJV**

who left his family when he was called, as did Jesus' disciples. . . .

### Matt 4:22 – *Following Jesus*

> 22 AND THEY IMMEDIATELY LEFT THE SHIP AND THEIR FATHER, AND FOLLOWED HIM. **KJV**

But the personality of Pharaoh does not know or fear Jehovah.

### Ex 5:2 – *Pharaoh Denies Jehovah*

> 2 AND PHARAOH SAID, **WHO IS THE LORD, THAT I SHOULD OBEY HIS VOICE TO LET ISRAEL GO?** I KNOW NOT THE LORD, NEITHER WILL I LET ISRAEL GO. **KJV**

Moses' separation from Zipporah and their children is an archetype, a universal crisis that is played out in this world, over and over, as husbands, wives and children resist God's call on the life of their mate, or parent.

In all fairness to the resisting family members who fight for the survival of their family, when God calls a family member, the family unit, as it exists at that time, is destroyed. It will never be the same again, even if the family member remains in the home.

### Matt 10:34-36 – *Jesus Divides*

> 34 THINK NOT THAT I AM COME TO SEND PEACE ON EARTH: **I CAME NOT TO SEND PEACE, BUT A SWORD.**
>
> 35 FOR I AM COME TO SET A MAN AT VARIANCE AGAINST **HIS FATHER, AND THE DAUGHTER AGAINST HER MOTHER, AND THE DAUGHTER IN LAW AGAINST HER MOTHER IN LAW.**
>
> 36 AND A MAN'S FOES SHALL BE THEY OF HIS OWN HOUSEHOLD. **KJV**

In the hour that Jehovah takes a man, or all of mankind, to serve the purpose for which he or they were created, and will wait for them no longer, . . .

### Rev 10:5-6 – *The End of Time*

> 5 AND THE ANGEL WHICH I SAW STAND UPON THE SEA AND UPON THE EARTH LIFTED UP HIS HAND TO HEAVEN,
>
> 6 AND SWARE BY HIM THAT LIVETH FOR EVER AND EVER, WHO CREATED HEAVEN, AND THE THINGS THAT THEREIN ARE, AND THE EARTH, AND THE THINGS THAT THEREIN ARE, AND THE SEA, AND THE THINGS WHICH ARE THEREIN, **THAT THERE SHOULD BE TIME NO LONGER: KJV**

every mortal who responds to the call will be converted and live, and everyone else will eventually die.

This great work is called *the Exodus*, and the Angel that separates the cattle from the cattle, physical man from physical man, . . .

### Matt 24:40 – *Two in the Field*

> 40 THEN SHALL **TWO BE IN THE FIELD**; THE ONE SHALL BE TAKEN, AND THE OTHER LEFT. **KJV**

is *the Lord Jesus Christ*, the only name by which men can be saved.

### Acts 4:12 – *No Salvation*

> 12 **NEITHER IS THERE SALVATION IN ANY OTHER:** FOR THERE IS NONE OTHER NAME UNDER HEAVEN GIVEN AMONG MEN, WHEREBY WE MUST BE SAVED. **KJV**

Zipporah refused to accept that everything in this world is temporary in relation to Jehovah, who abides beyond time, and that Jehovah's priorities pre-empt the most sacred of human ties in this world, those formed by marriage.

Jehovah claimed Moses for his own, and not only was Moses' marriage to Zipporah over, but Jehovah rejected their sons as well!

Moses was raised to a spiritual grade that is higher that human marriage.

**Mark 12:25** – *No Marriage*

25 FOR **WHEN THEY SHALL RISE FROM THE DEAD, THEY NEITHER MARRY, NOR ARE GIVEN IN MARRIAGE;** BUT ARE AS THE ANGELS WHICH ARE IN HEAVEN. **KJV**

Moses was to be joined to Aaron, a physically male partner, and their intimacy . . .

**2 Sam 1:26** – *Spiritual Intimacy*

26…**THY LOVE TO ME** WAS WONDERFUL, **PASSING THE LOVE OF WOMEN. KJV**

would be of spirit and mind, like Moses' intimacy with Joshua later on.[7]

**Ex 4:16** – *Moses & Aaron*

16 AND HE SHALL BE THY SPOKESMAN UNTO THE PEOPLE: AND HE SHALL BE, **EVEN HE SHALL BE TO THEE INSTEAD OF A MOUTH, AND THOU SHALT BE TO HIM INSTEAD OF GOD. KJV**

Some say that David was speaking about homosexual love, but this is not true.

**2 Sam 1:26** – *David and Jonathan*

26 I AM DISTRESSED FOR THEE, MY BROTHER JONATHAN: VERY PLEASANT HAST THOU BEEN UNTO ME: THY

---

[7] See, **Joshua, The Ethiopian Woman**, p 29

LOVE TO ME WAS WONDERFUL, PASSING THE LOVE OF WOMEN
**KJV**

The Scripture forbids homosexual behavior.

**<u>Lev 18:22</u>** – *Homosexuality Forbidden*

> 22 **THOU SHALT NOT LIE WITH MANKIND,** AS WITH WOMANKIND: IT IS ABOMINATION. **KJV**

# Marriage and Divorce

The child born of a marriage binds a man and woman for as long as they live. Neither party is ever fully divorced from the other, as long as a spiritual, emotional or mental connection with the child of the marriage, the fruit of their union, exists.

This truth is the spiritual basis for saying that a woman who remarries while her first husband is alive has two husbands, and is therefore an adulteress. . . .

**<u>Rom 7:3</u>** – *One Husband*

> 3 SO THEN **IF, WHILE HER HUSBAND LIVETH, SHE BE MARRIED TO ANOTHER MAN, SHE SHALL BE CALLED AN ADULTERESS**: BUT IF HER HUSBAND BE DEAD, SHE IS FREE FROM THAT LAW; SO THAT SHE IS NO ADULTERESS, THOUGH SHE BE MARRIED TO ANOTHER MAN. **KJV**

The tie with the first husband can only be broken through the death of the first husband, or the child.

Many have questioned why this restriction is for women only, and not men. The answer is that it applies to physical men as well as to physical woman, since all of humanity is spiritually female.

# Soul Marriage

The spiritual principle governing marriage and divorce can be expressed esoterically by attributing personal names to the spiritual organs of the couple that join together to form a new soul, a spiritual son, so to speak, who contains spiritual elements of both parties to the marriage. This soul, spiritual son, is the spiritual foundation upon which a physical child is eventually founded.

The man and the woman each have a dual, spiritual organ called Cain and Abel, which is capable of joining with Cain in their mate to form the new soul, the spiritual son that becomes the spiritual foundation of the marital unity.

This new soul is held to be as inviolable as a human child, itself, except that, unlike a physical child, it usually dies when the parties to the marriage divorce.

This new soul, the spiritual son of the marriage, can be so powerful, that sometimes it continues to exist in the mind and emotions of one partner, even after divorce or the death of their mate. In such an event, remarriage invariably fails, because the soul, or spiritual son, of the previous marriage, prevents the surviving spouse from forming a new soul, or spiritual son, with their new mate.

The shattering of the new soul, or spiritual son, that came into existence through the physical, mental, emotional and spiritual intimacy of the parties, is the death of the spiritual child, called *the soul of the marriage*, and the death of the marriage.

### *Cain Marries Cain*

In a human marriage, Cain, the animal natures of the mother and the father, join to form their spiritual son, the single soul that is the foundation of the marriage.

# Spiritual Marriage

## *Adam Marries Abel*

In a spiritual marriage between Jehovah and a mortal man, Jehovah's son, Adam, . . .

### Luke 3:38 – *Adam, the Son of God*

> 38 WHICH WAS THE SON OF ENOS, WHICH WAS THE SON OF SETH, WHICH WAS THE SON OF **ADAM, WHICH WAS THE SON OF GOD. KJV**

joins with Abel in the mortal man, to form a single soul, or spiritual son, the proof of intimacy between that man and God. This new soul is actually Adam, the Son of God, reborn, or regenerated, in that man.

In the New Testament, this new soul, the spiritual son of the marriage, is called *Christ*, and the mortal man that he exists in is called *a son of God*.

# Spiritual Circumcision

Abel is the spiritual manhood of mortal men, and Cain is Abel's foreskin.

## *The Metaphor*

The principle of *spiritual circumcision* is found in Saul's demand that David pay a dowry price of one hundred Philistine foreskins to marry his daughter, Michal.

**1 Sam 18:27** – *A Dowry of Foreskins*

> 27 WHEREFORE DAVID AROSE AND WENT, HE AND HIS
> MEN, AND SLEW OF THE PHILISTINES TWO HUNDRED MEN; **AND
> DAVID BROUGHT THEIR FORESKINS, AND THEY GAVE THEM
> IN FULL TALE TO THE KING,** THAT HE MIGHT BE THE KING'S
> SON IN LAW. AND SAUL GAVE HIM MICHAL HIS DAUGHTER TO
> WIFE. **KJV**

*One hundred* signifies the female spiritual power. Satan, the female power of the other side, was joined to Cain, the foreskin of Abel, the spiritual male power within the Philistines. The Philistines were spiritually completed men that the Bible calls *Nephilim*.

The Hebrew word translated, *slew*, means, *to beat* or *to strike*, and the Hebrew word translated, *he gave them in full tale*, means, *to be filled up*, or *complete.*

David did not bring one hundred pieces of bloody skin to Saul. David proved that he was spiritually and morally superior to the Philistines by defeating them in battle, without any harm to himself.

David delivered the defeated, completed Philistines, *the Nephilim*, to Saul, by stripping them of their spiritual power.

David, indeed, circumcised the Philistines. Righteous Adam within David, by the authority and strength of Jehovah Elohim, cut away the female power that defended their male mind of the Philistines, and brought them into submission to David's spiritual authority.

### 1 Sam 17:45-46 – *David & Goliath*

45 THEN SAID DAVID TO THE PHILISTINE, THOU COMEST TO ME WITH A SWORD, AND WITH A SPEAR, AND WITH A SHIELD: **BUT I COME TO THEE IN THE NAME OF THE LORD OF HOSTS, THE GOD OF THE ARMIES OF ISRAEL, WHOM THOU HAST DEFIED.**

46 **THIS DAY WILL THE LORD DELIVER THEE INTO MINE HAND**; AND I WILL SMITE THEE, AND TAKE THINE HEAD FROM THEE; AND I WILL GIVE THE CARCASES OF THE HOST OF THE PHILISTINES THIS DAY UNTO THE FOWLS OF THE AIR, AND TO THE WILD BEASTS OF THE EARTH; THAT ALL THE EARTH MAY KNOW THAT THERE IS A GOD IN ISRAEL. **KJV**

For those who are still doubtful that there is a spiritual circumcision, Jeremiah says clearly, that there is a spiritual circumcision of the heart, the seat of passion

### Jer 4:4 – *Circumcision of the Heart*

4 **CIRCUMCISE YOURSELVES** TO THE LORD, AND **TAKE AWAY THE FORESKINS OF YOUR HEART,** YE MEN OF JUDAH AND INHABITANTS OF JERUSALEM: LEST MY FURY COME FORTH LIKE FIRE, AND BURN THAT NONE CAN QUENCH IT, BECAUSE OF THE EVIL OF YOUR DOINGS. **KJV**

## *Abel's Spiritual Circumcision*

Adam joined to Abel in a man, is the mediator that connects that man to Jehovah's life-giving Spirit.

### 1 Tim 2:5 – *Christ Jesus, the Mediator*

5 FOR THERE IS ONE GOD, AND **ONE MEDIATOR BETWEEN GOD AND MEN**, THE MAN CHRIST JESUS; **KJV**

Cain, Abel's foreskin, lies on top of Abel in mortal men, so Abel must be circumcised before Adam, Jehovah's son, can marry him.

In other words, Cain must be cut away from Abel before Adam can join with Abel, to complete Jehovah's union with that man.

Whoever experiences spiritual circumcision (where Cain has been cut away and discarded), is now spiritually barren. That person is no longer emotionally or spiritually capable of forming the new soul, or spiritual son, that is the spiritual foundation of a human marriage. Cain, the organ of spiritual connection, no longer exists for that person.

This spiritual experience is called *the circumcision of Abel.*

*The circumcision of Abel* means that Adam, the son of God, cuts Cain away from the Cain-Abel unity in a man, and replaces Cain to bring the Jehovah-Abel unity into existence.[8]

## *Female, Physical Circumcision*

*The circumcision of Abel* is the spiritual type and shadow of physical, female circumcision, which barbaric practice is illegal in the Western World.

Physical, female circumcision is performed with the intent of destroying the woman's ability to enjoy sexual intercourse. It is, therefore, a permanent, surgical chastity belt.

Likewise, *the circumcision of Abel*, which is the cutting away of Cain, prevents the spiritual pleasure of emotional intimacy in marriage which results from the union of the two Cains, the animal, or emotional, nature of the parties. Spiritual intimacy with God is through union with his Spirit. God does not satisfy the animal emotions.

---

[8] See, also, *Moses' Spiritual Circumcision, p 49.*

**2 Peter 1:4** – *The Corruption of Lust*

4 WHEREBY ARE GIVEN UNTO US EXCEEDING GREAT AND PRECIOUS PROMISES: THAT BY THESE YE MIGHT BE PARTAKERS OF THE DIVINE NATURE, **HAVING ESCAPED THE CORRUPTION THAT IS IN THE WORLD THROUGH LUST. KJV**

## Moses' Spiritual Circumcision

Zipporah would not let go of Moses. He was so overtaken by his wife's witchcraft that he was taking her to Egypt, even though Jehovah told him not to. Years later, Ezra would have to tell the Jews returning to Jerusalem that they, too, had to leave their Babylonian wives and children behind.

**Ezra 10:2-3** – *Pagan Wives*

2 . . . WE HAVE . . . HAVE TAKEN STRANGE WIVES OF THE PEOPLE OF THE LAND: . . .

3 . . . **LET US . . . PUT AWAY ALL THE WIVES, AND SUCH AS ARE BORN OF THEM, ACCORDING TO THE COUNSEL OF MY LORD, . . . KJV**

# Moses' Marriage

## *On The Way to the Inn*

Jehovah's anger, the Sowing & Reaping Judgment, is not the prideful anger of mortal men. The Scripture that says that *Jehovah met Moses in the way and sought to kill <u>him</u>*, means that judgment was about to fall on *him*.

### Ex 4:24 – *Jehovah's Wrath*

> 24 AND IT CAME TO PASS BY THE WAY IN THE INN, THAT THE LORD MET HIM, **AND SOUGHT TO KILL HIM**. **KJV**

Now, if we are to understand what happened on the way to the inn, we need to know who *him* is. Is *him*, Moses? Zipporah? Gershom? Eliezer? or Moses' and Zipporah's spiritual son, the soul of the marriage that Zipporah would not give up?

## *Adam, Moses' New Mate*

Cain in Moses had to be cut away and discarded before Adam could marry Abel within Moses. But Cain within Moses was joined to Cain within Zipporah, and the two Cains, the spiritual foreskins of Moses and Zipporah, had become one new soul! Surely the cutting away of Cain within Moses would be the death of that new soul, the spiritual son which was the foundation of Moses' marriage to Zipporah!

Cain within Zipporah was holding on to Cain within Moses, and would not let go! Zipporah was enslaving Moses, binding him to herself, through sexual desire, emotional dependency and guilt about breaking their marriage vows and abandoning Gershom and Eliezer.

So, Jehovah spoke to Zipporah, saying, *withdraw Cain from Moses*. That is, release Moses sexually, emotionally and mentally, or Adam will circumcise Abel while Cain, your sexual, emotional and mental desire for each other, is intensified by your witchcraft.

Zipporah knew that if Jehovah made good his threat, Cain within herself, as well as Cain within Moses, would be cut away. Moses would not be harmed because Adam, Jehovah's circumcising knife, would join with Abel within Moses, but he would not marry Abel within Zipporah, who would become spiritually barren, a woman incapable of passion. In addition, Zipporah knew that she would lose her capacity to form a healthy and lasting bond with another man, which might result in an emotional and mental breakdown, and she might even die.

But, despite Jehovah's dire warning, Zipporah was still not willing to give Moses up, and sought to control him with guilt, saying, . . .

> **Ex 4:26 - AT: Moses, the Unfaithful Husband.** *You are ending a relationship that was meant to be permanent, which makes **you an unfaithful husband.*** **(ATB)**

Moses, you are an unfaithful husband and a bad father.

But Moses was in agreement with Jehovah that Abel should be circumcised and that he should marry Adam, so Moses continued to slip away from Zipporah's grasp.[9]

Then Zipporah tried to control Moses by stabbing him in his emotions, saying . . .

> **Ex 4:25 - AT: Moses' Spiritual Son.** *You are a husband that sheds the blood of his own [spiritual] son* **(ATB)**

---

[9] We can overcome any and all of Satan's seductions that have captured our soul, or emotions, by agreeing with Christ Jesus that we prefer him to anything that Satan can give us.

Then Zipporah seized her spiritual son, the emotional soul formed from her marriage to Moses, and severed Cain (who was covering Abel within Moses like a foreskin), the seat of her passion, and her spiritual, mental and emotional capacity to be intimate with another man, and withdrew him from Moses' spiritual universe.

# Moses and Aaron

### Ex 4:27-31 – *Moses Meets Aaron*

27 AND THE LORD SAID TO AARON, **GO INTO THE WILDERNESS TO MEET MOSES**. AND HE WENT, AND MET HIM IN THE MOUNT OF GOD, AND KISSED HIM.

28 **AND MOSES TOLD AARON ALL** THE WORDS OF THE LORD WHO HAD SENT HIM, AND ALL THE SIGNS WHICH HE HAD COMMANDED HIM.

29 AND MOSES AND AARON WENT AND GATHERED TOGETHER ALL THE ELDERS OF THE CHILDREN OF ISRAEL:

30 AND AARON SPAKE ALL THE WORDS WHICH THE LORD HAD SPOKEN UNTO MOSES, AND DID THE SIGNS IN THE SIGHT OF THE PEOPLE.

31 AND THE PEOPLE BELIEVED: AND WHEN THEY HEARD THAT THE LORD HAD VISITED THE CHILDREN OF ISRAEL, AND THAT HE HAD LOOKED UPON THEIR AFFLICTION, THEN THEY BOWED THEIR HEADS AND WORSHIPPED. **KJV**

Jehovah spoke to Aaron, who was still in Egypt with his family, and caught him up into the spiritually high place that Moses had already ascended to. The souls of Moses and Aaron met there in that high place, and kissed, or blended together, and in that union of mind, Moses' soul gave Aaron's soul the information concerning their upcoming meeting in Egypt, and the details of their future relationship.

# Moses and Jethro

The Scripture says that Jethro sacrificed to Jehovah, so some believe that Jethro converted to Judaism. But Jethro was a Midianite, a worshipper of multiple gods, and the God of Abraham, the father of Midian by Keturah, Moses' second wife, was not unknown to him.

The truth of the matter is that the Scripture says that Jethro sacrificed to *God*. It does not say that Jethro sacrificed to Jehovah (the Lord).

Jethro praised Jehovah . . .

> **Ex 18:10-11** *– Jethro Praises Jehovah*
>
> 10 AND JETHRO SAID, BLESSED BE THE LORD, **WHO HATH DELIVERED YOU OUT OF THE HAND OF THE EGYPTIANS,** AND OUT OF THE HAND OF PHARAOH, WHO HATH DELIVERED THE PEOPLE FROM UNDER THE HAND OF THE EGYPTIANS.
>
> 11 NOW I KNOW THAT **THE LORD IS GREATER THAN ALL GODS:** FOR IN THE THING WHEREIN THEY DEALT PROUDLY HE WAS ABOVE THEM. **KJV**

after which he sacrificed to *God* . . .

> **Ex 18:12** *– Jethro's Sacrifice*
>
> 12 **AND JETHRO, MOSES' FATHER IN LAW, TOOK A BURNT OFFERING AND SACRIFICES FOR GOD:** AND AARON CAME, AND ALL THE ELDERS OF ISRAEL, TO EAT BREAD WITH MOSES' FATHER IN LAW BEFORE GOD. **KJV**

but we don't know which God. Some assume that it was Jehovah, because Jethro praises Jehovah in the previous verse, but that is an assumption without a foundation.

There is no evidence that Jethro sacrificed to Jehovah, or converted, or was circumcised. Neither does the Scripture say anything about Zipporah converting, or Jehovah telling Jethro to bring Zipporah and the children back to Moses.

Jethro's technique of praising Jehovah and then sacrificing to some unidentified god is a typical antichrist technique. First, antichrist says something true, which puts the victim off guard. Then he follows it up quickly with a lie, and the dupe swallows down both the truth and the lie in one gulp.

On the other hand, it was common in Bible days for people, even high priests, to abandon the gods they served, to worship other gods who they perceived to have more power. But this was not Jethro's motive for sacrificing to Jehovah, if he did, indeed, sacrifice to Jehovah.

To give Jethro the benefit of the doubt, it is possible that he did, indeed, in his mind, sacrifice to Jehovah. But the fact that the Scripture says that Jethro sacrificed to *God*, tells it all. Even if Jethro had Jehovah in mind, he was so spiritually polygamous from worshipping multiple gods all of his life, that any thoughts of Jehovah were swallowed up by the idolatrous mass of mixed spirituality already existing in his mind.

### *Jethro's Counsel*

The very next day after Jethro acknowledged that the God of Israel was more powerful than all the other gods, Jethro presumed to be wise enough to counsel Moses!

**Ex 18:19** – *Jethro Counsels Moses*

> 19 HEARKEN NOW UNTO MY VOICE, I WILL GIVE THEE COUNSEL, AND GOD SHALL BE WITH THEE: BE THOU FOR THE PEOPLE TO GODWARD, THAT THOU MAYEST BRING THE CAUSES UNTO GOD: **KJV**

Amazing as it may be, Moses the man of God, the only Mediator between Jehovah and Israel . . .

### 1 Cor 10:2 – *Baptized Into Moses*

> 2 AND **WERE ALL BAPTIZED UNTO MOSES** IN THE CLOUD AND IN THE SEA; **KJV**

who Jehovah spoke to, face to face, . . .

### Ex 33:11 –*Jehovah Speaks To Moses*

> 11 AND **THE LORD** SPAKE UNTO MOSES FACE TO FACE, AS A MAN SPEAKETH UNTO HIS FRIEND. AND HE TURNED AGAIN INTO THE CAMP: BUT HIS SERVANT JOSHUA, THE SON OF NUN, A YOUNG MAN, DEPARTED NOT OUT OF THE TABERNACLE. **KJV**

accepted Jethro, a brand-new convert, so to speak, as mediator between Jehovah and himself, and received Jethro's counsel!

### Ex 18:24 – *Moses Obeys Jethro*

> 24 SO **MOSES HEARKENED TO THE VOICE OF HIS FATHER IN LAW,** AND DID ALL THAT HE HAD SAID. **KJV**

Jethro spoke in the name of Elohim, God, not in the name of Jehovah, Lord, and the Scripture does not say which God Jethro was speaking for . . .

### Ex 18:23 –*Unidentified God*

> 23 IF THOU SHALT DO THIS THING, **AND GOD COMMAND THEE SO,** THEN THOU SHALT BE ABLE TO ENDURE, AND ALL THIS PEOPLE SHALL ALSO GO TO THEIR PLACE IN PEACE. **KJV**

### 1 Cor 8:5 – *Many Gods*

> 5 FOR THOUGH THERE BE THAT ARE CALLED GODS,
> WHETHER IN HEAVEN OR IN EARTH, (AS THERE BE GODS
> MANY, AND LORDS MANY,)  **KJV**

apparently, Moses, and many Bible scholars as well, have assumed that Jethro was speaking on behalf of Jehovah.

Jehovah spoke to Moses face to face, so it is reasonable to assume that Moses was following Jehovah's direct instructions when Jethro, moved by a strange god, took authority over Moses.

Jehovah gave Solomon wisdom and an understanding heart . .

### 1 Kings 3:12 – *Wise and Understanding Heart*

> 12 BEHOLD, I HAVE DONE ACCORDING TO THY
> WORDS: LO, **I HAVE GIVEN THEE A WISE AND AN**
> **UNDERSTANDING HEART**; SO THAT THERE WAS NONE LIKE
> THEE BEFORE THEE, NEITHER AFTER THEE SHALL ANY ARISE
> LIKE UNTO THEE. **KJV**

to judge the people, and we have every reason to believe that he gave Moses the same tools. Jehovah fully equipped Moses to do the job at hand. Aaron was Moses' only God-ordained assistant.

Jethro ignored Moses' relationship with Jehovah, and overrode Jehovah's instructions, to tell Moses that what he was doing was *no good, and too hard to perform alone.* . . .

### Ex 18:18 – *Jethro's Counsel - 1*

> 18 **THOU WILT SURELY WEAR AWAY, BOTH THOU,**
> **AND THIS PEOPLE THAT IS WITH THEE: FOR THIS THING IS**
> **TOO HEAVY FOR THEE; THOU ART NOT ABLE TO PERFORM**
> **IT THYSELF ALONE.** **KJV**

Moses was not alone. Jehovah spoke to him face to face. In addition, there was Aaron, and Miriam, and the Elders of Israel.

Do you really believe that Jehovah spoke to Moses through a Midianite priest? Not a chance, brethren!

Jethro denied Moses' ability and authority to judge the people. He advised Moses to function like the pagan oracles who present the people's petitions to their god, and then repeat their responses to the people.

**Ex 18:19** – *Jethro's Counsel - 2*

> 19 NOW LISTEN, AND LET ME GIVE YOU A WORD OF ADVICE, AND GOD WILL BLESS YOU: BE THESE PEOPLE'S LAWYER-THEIR REPRESENTATIVE BEFORE GOD-**BRINGING HIM THEIR QUESTIONS TO DECIDE; YOU WILL TELL THEM HIS DECISIONS,** *TEACHING THEM GOD'S LAWS,* AND *SHOWING THEM THE PRINCIPLES OF GODLY LIVING.* **TLB**

Jehovah gave Moses the wisdom to judge the people. Moses did not channel the petitions of the people and Jehovah's responses.

It is interesting to note the reappearance of Jethro's antichrist spirit in verse 19. Jethro destroys Moses' authority as a judge, and in the very same verse, Jethro affirms Moses' commission *to teach God's laws* and to *show the people the principles of good living*.

Jethro told Moses to appoint men who feared God, men of truth, who hated covetousness, to judge the people, but Jethro did not say which God they should fear, or whose truth they should believe. Also, Jethro mentions hatred for covetousness, a quality that one would look for in a ruler, antichrist confusion again.

**Ex 18:21** – *Jethro's Counsel - 3*

> 21 MOREOVER THOU SHALT PROVIDE OUT OF ALL THE PEOPLE **ABLE MEN, SUCH AS FEAR GOD, MEN OF TRUTH,** *HATING COVETOUSNESS*; AND PLACE SUCH OVER THEM, TO BE RULERS OF THOUSANDS, AND RULERS OF HUNDREDS, RULERS OF FIFTIES, AND RULERS OF TENS: **KJV**

## *Moses Seduced*

Moses made the same mistake that the woman in the Garden made, that other prophets made after him, and that Sons of God are still making today: They obey the word of another man, rather than the Word that the Lord spoke to them face to face.

### 1 Kings 13:18, 24, 26 – *Another Prophet*

18 HE SAID UNTO HIM, I AM A PROPHET ALSO AS THOU ART; AND AN ANGEL SPAKE UNTO ME BY THE WORD OF THE LORD, SAYING, BRING HIM BACK WITH THEE INTO THINE HOUSE, THAT HE MAY EAT BREAD AND DRINK WATER. BUT HE LIED UNTO HIM.

24 AND WHEN HE WAS GONE, A LION MET HIM BY THE WAY, AND SLEW HIM: AND HIS CARCASE WAS CAST IN THE WAY, AND THE ASS STOOD BY IT, THE LION ALSO STOOD BY THE CARCASE.

26 AND WHEN THE PROPHET THAT BROUGHT HIM BACK FROM THE WAY HEARD THEREOF, HE SAID, IT IS THE MAN OF GOD, WHO WAS DISOBEDIENT UNTO THE WORD OF THE LORD: THEREFORE THE LORD HATH DELIVERED HIM UNTO THE LION, WHICH HATH TORN HIM, AND SLAIN HIM, ACCORDING TO THE WORD OF THE LORD, WHICH HE SPAKE UNTO HIM. **KJV**

It is also interesting to note that Moses' reiterates Jethro's counsel . . .

### Num 11:14-15 – *Moses' Self-Pity*

14 I AM NOT ABLE TO BEAR ALL THIS PEOPLE ALONE, BECAUSE IT IS TOO HEAVY FOR ME.

15 AND IF THOU DEAL THUS WITH ME, KILL ME, I PRAY THEE, OUT OF HAND, IF I HAVE FOUND FAVOUR IN THY SIGHT; AND LET ME NOT SEE MY WRETCHEDNESS. **KJV**

Who has the vision to see how Jethro's serpentine counsel corrupted Moses and reduced that man of God, who had a face-to-face relationship with Jehovah, into a quivering mass of negativity?

Let's compare Jehovah and Jethro's words . . .

### Num 11:16-17 – *Jehovah's Solution*

16 AND THE LORD SAID UNTO MOSES, **GATHER UNTO ME** SEVENTY MEN OF **THE ELDERS OF ISRAEL WHOM THOU KNOWEST TO BE THE ELDERS OF THE PEOPLE, AND OFFICERS OVER THEM; AND BRING THEM UNTO THE TABERNACLE OF THE CONGREGATION, THAT THEY MAY STAND THERE WITH THEE.**

17 AND I WILL TAKE OF THE SPIRIT WHICH IS UPON THEE, AND WILL PUT IT UPON THEM; AND THEY SHALL BEAR THE BURDEN OF THE PEOPLE WITH THEE, THAT THOU BEAR IT NOT THYSELF ALONE. **KJV**

| Jehovah | Jethro |
|---|---|
| Gather unto me 70 men | You provide |
| Elders of Israel | Out of all the people |
| Whom thou knowest to be the elders of the people, | Able men, such as fear God, men of truth, hating covetousness |
| And [put] officers over them | And place such over them [no check or balance over the rulers] |
| And bring them unto the tabernacle of the congregation, that they may stand there with you | To be rulers [no mention of God, or shared powers with Moses. Jethro advises Moses to turn all power and authority over to these men with no oversight] |

Jethro's counsel was for Moses to choose men out of his own understanding, but Jehovah's solution was to give those men *His Spirit*, the same Spirit that qualified and equipped Moses to do the job!

### *Jethro's Motives*

Jethro was a pagan high priest. Jethro knew that his daughter's marriage ended when Jehovah told Moses to leave his idolatress wife, but Jethro brought her and their children to Moses anyway. Why?

It is interesting to note that Jethro came to Moses immediately after Amalek attacked Israel and was defeated by Joshua and the Hebrew army. . . .

<u>Ex 17:13</u> *–Amalek Discomforted*

> 13 AND JOSHUA DISCOMFITED AMALEK AND HIS PEOPLE WITH THE EDGE OF THE SWORD. **KJV**

forty years later, Moab and Midian would commission Balaam to destroy Israel . . .

<u>Num 22:4-5</u> – *Balak Commissions Moses*

> 4 AND MOAB SAID UNTO THE ELDERS OF MIDIAN, NOW SHALL THIS COMPANY LICK UP ALL THAT ARE ROUND ABOUT US, AS THE OX LICKETH UP THE GRASS OF THE FIELD. AND BALAK THE SON OF ZIPPOR WAS KING OF THE MOABITES AT THAT TIME.
>
> 5 HE SENT MESSENGERS THEREFORE UNTO BALAAM THE SON OF BEOR TO PETHOR . . . . **KJV**

and, failing to do so, sent their woman to seduce the Israelite men.

Considering this, is it so far out to think that Jethro came to Moses to weaken him, both out of retaliation for abandoning Zipporah and to protect Midian from Israel? Was Jethro seeking to do the same thing that Moab and Midian sought to do 40 years later?

Jethro brought Zipporah and her children to Moses in the wilderness because the Midianite god within him, the Jezebel within Jethro, told him to do so, for the very same reason that Balak and the King of Midian commissioned Balaam.

We hear no more of Zipporah, Gershom and Elizer, except for those who believe that Zipporah was the Ethiopian woman. So, Zipporah and the children must have returned to Midian with Jethro.

## Moses, a Eunuch For God

Jehovah tells the men of Israel to abstain from sexual activities with their wives . . .

### Ex 19:15 – *Come Not At Your Wives*

> 15 AND HE SAID UNTO THE PEOPLE, BE READY AGAINST THE THIRD DAY: **COME NOT AT YOUR WIVES. KJV**

to prepare themselves to receive Jehovah's offer of a Covenant.

The Hebrew idiom *tent*, suggests that a man's wife is his tent because he lives inside of her, both sexually and emotionally. . . .

### Gen 2:23 – *Bone of My Bones*

> 23 AND ADAM SAID, **THIS IS NOW BONE OF MY BONES, AND FLESH OF MY FLESH: SHE SHALL BE CALLED WOMAN,** BECAUSE SHE WAS TAKEN OUT OF MAN. **KJV**

### Eph 5:31 – *One Flesh*

> 31 FOR THIS CAUSE SHALL A MAN LEAVE HIS FATHER AND MOTHER, AND SHALL BE JOINED UNTO HIS WIFE, AND **THEY TWO SHALL BE ONE FLESH. KJV**

Also, a married man's wisdom is inside of his wife directing her, and watching over her when he is not physically present.

At some point, Jehovah said to the men of Israel, ***Go back to your tents***, meaning, ***Go back to your natural lives where you live inside of your wives***. But he did not say that to Moses. Jehovah did not tell Moses to go back to his tent, because Moses had ascended to a spiritual place that is higher than the physical life.

Moses was married to God.

# IV.

# CHRISTIAN ISRAEL

# IV.
# CHRISTIAN ISRAEL

## Christ

In the New Testament, we see that the fused DNA of Nimrod and Abraham's Israel, is called Christ, Abraham's seed.

<u>Gal 3:16</u> – *Promised Seed*

> 16 NOW TO **ABRAHAM AND HIS SEED WERE THE PROMISES MADE.** HE SAITH NOT, AND TO SEEDS, AS OF MANY; BUT AS OF ONE, **AND TO THY SEED, WHICH IS CHRIST.** **KJV**

Christ, *the promised seed*, matured into Righteous Adam, Jesus of Nazareth's inner man . . .

<u>Eph 3:16</u> – *Inner Man*

> 16 THAT HE WOULD GRANT YOU, ACCORDING TO THE RICHES OF HIS GLORY, TO BE STRENGTHENED WITH MIGHT BY HIS SPIRIT IN THE INNER MAN; **KJV**

and

Righteous Adam within Jesus, married the spirit of Elijah by whom Jesus overcame death, and

the spirit of Elijah,

Righteous Adam,[10] the only Mediator between God and man, and

the man, Jesus of Nazareth,

blended together and became one glorified man called ***the Lord Jesus Christ***.

Today, the spiritual seed of the glorified Jesus Christ is grafting to the individual members of the Church of Jesus Christ, in the same manner that the genetic and spiritual greatness of Seth within Nimrod's Black Israel, fused with Abraham's Israel, a tribe of shepherds.

Christ, Abraham's seed, is fusing his genetic and spiritual DNA with many ordinary human beings, male, female, Jew, Greek, black, white and every other color, who have received Jesus Christ as their Lord and Savior.

The people are ordinary, but the seed of the Lord Jesus Christ contains the genetic and spiritual greatness of Seth that was in Black Israel, and Abraham's DNA, which carries the potential to produce the righteous nature and the immortal bodies . . .

### Heb 7:16 – *Endless Life*

> 16 WHO IS MADE, NOT AFTER THE LAW OF A CARNAL COMMANDMENT, BUT AFTER **THE POWER OF AN ENDLESS LIFE. KJV**

promised to Abraham's Israel.

Christ is one seed, but he is a many-membered seed.

---

[10] Righteous Adam in is called ***Christ Jesus*** in the New Testament.

# SPIRITUAL ISRAEL

Spiritual Israel is a company of heavenly beings who have been influencing mankind for a long time. They were incarnate in Nimrod's Israel, and Abraham's Israel, in the people who followed Moses out of Egypt, and, more recently, in Christian Israel. Soon, they will appear again as

Christ Jesus, the only mediator between God and man, who is

The husband of the Church, and

### **Eph 5:23** – *Head of the Church*

23 FOR THE HUSBAND IS THE HEAD OF THE WIFE, EVEN AS CHRIST IS THE HEAD OF THE CHURCH: AND HE IS THE SAVIOUR OF THE BODY. **KJV**

*The new, Inner Man of the Israel of God.*

## Spiritual Israel in Judah

Spiritual Israel appeared in Judah, the remnant of Abraham's Israel, two thousand years ago, as Jesus, the Christ. But Judah's Rulers rejected Jesus, so Christ remained only with the individual Judeans who recognized Jesus as Messiah.

Spiritual events come to pass slowly. The withdrawal of spiritual Israel from one nation (Judah) and its incarnation in another nation (the Church) takes time, and, indeed, two thousand years have passed since Herod's temple was destroyed.

# Spiritual Israel in the Church

Spiritual Israel is appearing in the Church today through Christ Jesus, the spiritual son of Jesus Christ. The Church is nationally diverse and does not have a tribal identity. Some believe, however, despite the fact that Christ is given for all, that the genetic descendants of Japheth and Abraham are particularly attracted to her.

# Spiritual Israel in Modern-Day Jewry

Some modern-day, observant Jews, still experience what the Rabbis call, ***bonding to Jehovah***, which means that they have a relationship with the God of the Bible.

### *A Testimony*

The Lord revealed Himself to me, a 10-year-old Jewish girl, during Saturday morning services at the Synagogue where I took Hebrew lessons. I didn't understand what I was experiencing at the time, but I missed it enough to look for that *feeling* for years, until I found it again in a Pentecostal church.

### *Bound To God*

How do we bond to God? The Spirit of God is in the Scripture, the Word of God. We bond to him by responding to his Spirit. It is not necessary to know God's Name. He will reveal His Name in due season . . .

### Gen 17:1 – *Almighty God & Abraham*

> 1 AND WHEN ABRAM WAS NINETY YEARS OLD AND
> NINE, THE LORD APPEARED TO ABRAM, AND SAID UNTO HIM, **I
> AM THE ALMIGHTY GOD** [EL SHADDAI]; WALK BEFORE ME,
> AND BE THOU PERFECT. **KJV**

to the one seeking Him.

Fervent, persistent and passionate study of the Scripture draws the Spirit of God, the author of the Word of God, to the student. After that, the Spirit of God bonds to the student

## A Mediator for the Jew

Jewish people will tell you that they do not have or need a mediator, but that is not true. The Jewish people have always sought communication with and been taught by angels. Their own Scripture says so. The prophets are also mediators. King Hezekiah sent Eliakim and Shebna to Isaiah, to ask Jehovah if He would intercede on behalf of Judah.

### 2 Kings 19:2 – *Israel's Mediators*

> 2 AND **HE SENT ELIAKIM**, WHICH WAS OVER THE
> HOUSEHOLD, AND SHEBNA THE SCRIBE, AND THE ELDERS OF
> THE PRIESTS, **COVERED WITH SACKCLOTH, TO ISAIAH THE
> PROPHET** THE SON OF AMOZ. **KJV**

And what about Moses?

### 1 Cor 10:2 – *Baptized Into Moses*

> 2 AND **WERE ALL BAPTIZED UNTO MOSES** IN THE
> CLOUD AND IN THE SEA; **KJV**

Also, it is a common practice for many ultra-orthodox Jews today to pray at the gravesite of their dead rabbi. They believe that the soul of the rabbi remains close to the rabbi's dead bones, and is, at the same time, also in the presence of God. So they seek intercession, a channel to God, at their rabbi's grave.

There are Jews who are crying out to Jehovah, as they understand him, today, and he is responding because their heart is cleaving, not so much to the Law or the rituals (although they do *keep the law*), but to their God.

### Ps 22:3 – *Praises of Israel*

> 3 BUT THOU ART HOLY, O THOU THAT INHABITEST THE PRAISES OF ISRAEL. KJV

Are they touching and drawing down the Spirit of Jehovah, or spiritual Israel, or angels, or are they touching the Lord Jesus? Who is it that responds? It is most likely that the Holy Spirit of Jesus Christ, because Jehovah is speaking through the Spirit of His Son today.

### Heb 1:1-2 – *God Speaks Through His Son*

> 1 GOD, WHO AT SUNDRY TIMES AND IN DIVERS MANNERS SPAKE IN TIME PAST UNTO THE FATHERS BY THE PROPHETS,
>
> 2 HATH IN THESE LAST DAYS SPOKEN UNTO US BY HIS SON, WHOM HE HATH APPOINTED HEIR OF ALL THINGS, BY WHOM ALSO HE MADE THE WORLDS; KJV

The Scripture says that Jesus comes as a thief in the night, that is, unknown to the one He is visiting.

### 1 Thess 5:2 – *A Thief In The Night*

> 2 FOR YOURSELVES KNOW PERFECTLY THAT THE DAY OF THE LORD SO COMETH AS A THIEF IN THE NIGHT. KJV

# THE ISRAEL OF GOD

The Israel of God is Christ Jesus, the complete, many-membered spiritual man. He is appearing as the New Man of the Body of Christ through the many members of the believers who host Him.

### Eph 2:15 – *One New Man*

15 HAVING ABOLISHED IN HIS FLESH THE ENMITY, EVEN THE LAW OF COMMANDMENTS CONTAINED IN ORDINANCES; FOR TO MAKE IN HIMSELF OF TWAIN **ONE NEW MAN, SO MAKING PEACE**; **KJV**

## The Man, Christ Jesus

The man, Christ Jesus, is the only mediator between God and Man.

### 1 Tim 2:5 – *One Mediator*

5 FOR THERE IS ONE GOD, AND **ONE MEDIATOR BETWEEN GOD AND MEN**, THE MAN CHRIST JESUS; **KJV**

### *Kings and Priests*

The people that Christ appears in are kings who establish and enforce the Rule of Law . . .

### Rev 1:6 – *Kings and Priests*

> 6 AND **HATH MADE US KINGS AND PRIESTS** UNTO GOD AND HIS FATHER; TO HIM BE GLORY AND DOMINION FOR EVER AND EVER. AMEN. **KJV**

and priests, who bring the petitions of the people before God.

The people of the Israel of God become kings when Christ Jesus, their inner man, draws the citizens of the kingdom to them.

Israel traditionally chooses their king, . . .

### 1 Kings 12:20 – *Israel's Choice*

> 20 AND IT CAME TO PASS, WHEN ALL ISRAEL HEARD THAT JEROBOAM WAS COME AGAIN, THAT **THEY SENT AND CALLED HIM UNTO THE CONGREGATION, AND MADE HIM KING OVER ALL ISRAEL**: THERE WAS NONE THAT FOLLOWED THE HOUSE OF DAVID, BUT THE TRIBE OF JUDAH ONLY. **KJV**

and so it is with the Israel of God. They follow only the leaders that Christ Jesus directs them to.

## *Jesus' Male Child*

Christ Jesus is the spiritual male offspring of the Lord Jesus Christ and the Church . . .

### Rev 12:5 – *A Man Child*

> 5 AND **SHE BROUGHT FORTH A MAN CHILD**, WHO WAS TO RULE ALL NATIONS WITH A ROD OF IRON: AND HER CHILD WAS CAUGHT UP UNTO GOD, AND TO HIS THRONE. **KJV**

Jesus is the Son of God . . .

<u>**Mark 1:1**</u> *– Christ Jesus*

1 THE BEGINNING OF THE GOSPEL OF **JESUS CHRIST, THE SON OF GOD**; **KJV**

## *The Lamb of God*

Christ Jesus is the extension of the Son of God in the believer. He is the spiritual part of the believer that the Lord Jesus joins himself to in marriage.

<u>**Rev 19:7**</u> *- Marriage of the Lamb*

7 LET US BE GLAD AND REJOICE, AND GIVE HONOUR TO HIM: FOR **THE MARRIAGE OF THE LAMB IS COME,** AND HIS WIFE HATH MADE HERSELF READY. **KJV**

Christ Jesus is the regenerated Adam.

The union of the Lord Jesus Christ in heaven and Christ Jesus in the earth, joins Heaven and Earth. Their unity destroys the powers and principalities . . .

<u>**Eph 6:12**</u> *– Principalities & Powers*

12 FOR WE WRESTLE NOT AGAINST FLESH AND BLOOD, BUT AGAINST **PRINCIPALITIES, AGAINST POWERS, AGAINST THE RULERS OF THE DARKNESS OF THIS WORLD, AGAINST SPIRITUAL WICKEDNESS IN HIGH PLACES. KJV**

that have dominated mankind since the female Adam committed adultery with the Serpent.

# EUROPE IS

## Israel

### British Israel

The doctrine of British Israel teaches that the royal family of England descends from the tribe of Judah through three princesses, the daughters of King Zedekiah of Judah.

These three princesses were the granddaughters of Jeremiah, who fled with them to Ireland after Nebuchadnezzar razed Judah and took the seed royal to Babylon.

The Scripture says that Jeremiah fled to Egypt, but *British Israel* says that Jeremiah escaped to the British Isles *after* he went to Egypt.

*British Israel* also teaches that the ten lost tribes of Israel's Northern Kingdom are not really lost, but exist today as the nations of Europe.

Denmark appears to have been settled by the tribe of Dan, for example, as well as Ireland where *Daniel* is as common as the name *John*.

## Anti-Semitic

The question of Europe's spiritual root surfaced years ago, when it became evident how much hatred the European nations have towards modern-day Israel. Why would that be? Why is there so much anti-Semitism extending from the European nations towards modern-day Israel?

The ten tribes of the Northern Kingdom warred against Judah, the Southern Kingdom, from time to time, but was the enmity so great that it resurfaced in Europe in a future century as the anti-semetic rage that reached its zenith in Hitler's Germany?

# Esau . . . .

### *According to the Rabbis*

The Rabbis of today say that Europe, but mostly Rome, is Esau, Isaac's son, who sold his birthright to his brother, Jacob, for food.

**Heb 12:16** – *Esau's Birthright*

> 16 LEST THERE BE ANY FORNICATOR, OR PROFANE PERSON, AS ESAU, WHO **FOR ONE MORSEL OF MEAT SOLD HIS BIRTHRIGHT. KJV**

After that, Jacob acquired Esau's blessing, as well, by impersonating Esau and deceiving Isaac, his father.

**Gen 27:36** – *Esau's Blessing*

> 36 AND HE SAID, IS NOT HE RIGHTLY NAMED JACOB? FOR HE HATH SUPPLANTED ME THESE TWO TIMES: **HE TOOK AWAY MY BIRTHRIGHT; AND, BEHOLD, NOW HE HATH TAKEN AWAY MY BLESSING.** AND HE SAID, HAST THOU NOT RESERVED A BLESSING FOR ME? **KJV**

So, the European nations appear to be Esau . . . .

Some say that European Esau hates Jacob with such a passion, and has such a murderous, anti-Semitic spirit towards Israel, because

Jacob acquired Esau's inheritance, his heritage, his birthright, and his blessing.

Others say that a subtle memory of Jacob stealing Esau's birthright and spiritual inheritance, is burned in the collective unconscious of European Esau. They say that that memory justifies European Esau's hatred for modern-day Israel and the Jewish people who live in Europe.

The problem here is, if Esau hates Jacob, he must hate all of Jacob's children, that is, all twelve tribes, not only the tribe of Judah. The animosity and the warfare that has raged between the European nations for centuries, in addition to European anti-Semitism, might be evidence Esau's influence on the European nations, to destroy themselves.

# ESAU AND JACOB

## At The River Jabbok

Jacob fled from Esau's wrath after he acquired Esau's blessing by deceiving Isaac. Now that Jacob was on his way home, he was afraid that Esau might still have deadly intentions towards him.

### Gen 27:41 – *Esau's Deadly Intentions*

> 41 AND ESAU HATED JACOB BECAUSE OF THE BLESSING WHEREWITH HIS FATHER BLESSED HIM: AND ESAU SAID IN HIS HEART, THE DAYS OF MOURNING FOR MY FATHER ARE AT HAND; **THEN WILL I SLAY MY BROTHER JACOB. KJV**

Jacob's caravan had already crossed the river Jabbok, which bordered on Esau's territory . . .

### Gen 32:22 – *Jacob Crosses The Jabbok*

> 22 AND HE ROSE UP THAT NIGHT, AND TOOK HIS TWO WIVES, AND HIS TWO WOMEN SERVANTS, AND HIS ELEVEN SONS, **AND PASSED OVER THE FORD JABBOK. KJV**

and Jacob knew that he would have to face Esau in the morning.

The night before Jacob's dreaded encounter with his brother, Esau, Jacob struggled within himself to find the mind, counsel and strength of God.

### *Jacob's Double Trouble*

The rabbis say that Jacob wrestled with Esau's angel. This is true, but Jacob wrestled against his own angel, his carnal mind, as well.

Both angels, the carnal minds of the two brothers, sought to prevent Righteous Adam from rising within Jacob.

*Righteous Adam* is Jacob's Righteous side, which includes the mind of God within Jacob. *Righteous Adam* is called *the man, Christ Jesus*, in the New Testament.

### 1 Tim 2:5 – *The Man*

> 5 FOR THERE IS ONE GOD, AND ONE MEDIATOR BETWEEN GOD AND MEN, THE MAN CHRIST JESUS; **KJV**

Righteous Adam was full well able to give Jacob the victory over Esau, despite the odds, if he could only rise above Jacob's fear of Esau. Jacob would have to face Esau on his own, without the help of God, if he could not overcome his fears.

> **Is 14:19 - AT: Jacob's carnal mind**. *But you, the abominable root [of fallen mankind], are cast out of the human bodies that you dress yourself in, which you slew **when you thrust [Adam, their Righteous mind], through with false doctrine**, [who Satan] forced down [into the lower parts of] Sheol, [where they are confused] stones [suspended in a mind of unconstructed consciousness]* **(ATB)**

## Laban & Jacob's Fear

Jacob was a strong man, but after experiencing Laban, his father-in-law's betrayal and injustice for so many years, he had become fearful. Jacob had a bad moment. He was so frightened of Esau[11] that Jacob's Righteous side, the spiritual man within him that connects him to God, could not rise above Jacob's carnal mind . . .

---

[11] One of the translations for the word *Jabbok*, is *overwhelmed*. Jacob was overwhelmed.

Rom 8:7 – *The carnal mind*

> 7 BECAUSE THE CARNAL MIND IS ENMITY AGAINST
> GOD: FOR IT IS NOT SUBJECT TO THE LAW OF GOD, NEITHER
> INDEED CAN BE. **KJV**

to engage Esau's angel (inner man, or carnal mind), in battle.

At first Jacob struggled within himself, his two sides opposing each other, Righteous Adam against Jacob's carnal mind, until Righteous *Adam* wounded Jacob's other side . . .

**Gen 32:25** – *Jacob's Thigh*

> 25 AND WHEN HE SAW THAT HE PREVAILED NOT
> AGAINST HIM, **HE TOUCHED THE HOLLOW OF HIS THIGH; AND**
> **THE HOLLOW OF JACOB'S THIGH WAS OUT OF JOINT,** AS HE
> WRESTLED WITH HIM. **KJV**

and Righteous Adam emerged as the victor over the fears of Jacob's carnal mind.

**Gen 32:24** – *Jacob & The Man*

> 24 AND JACOB WAS LEFT ALONE; **AND THERE**
> **WRESTLED A MAN WITH HIM UNTIL THE BREAKING OF THE**
> **DAY. KJV**

### *Victory Over Esau*

Now that the struggle would be between Righteous Adam and Esau's carnal mind, rather than between the carnal minds of the two men, the victory over Esau's carnal mind was assured.

Righteous Adam overshadowed Esau, and forced him to make peace with Jacob, and Esau let Jacob pass into Esau's territory safely . . .

<u>Gen 33:4</u> – *Esau Embraces Jacob*

> 4 AND ESAU RAN TO MEET HIM, AND EMBRACED HIM, AND FELL ON HIS NECK, AND KISSED HIM: AND THEY WEPT. **KJV**

But, Esau's carnal mind was only temporarily overshadowed. After Jacob was safely home, Righteous Adam took His hand off of Esau, . . .

<u>John 13:27</u> – *Satan Enters Judas*

> 27 AND AFTER THE SOP **SATAN ENTERED INTO HIM. THEN SAID JESUS UNTO HIM, THAT THOU DOEST, DO QUICKLY.** **KJV**

and Esau's hatred returned, and remains until this very day.

After that, Adam, Jacob's righteous, inner man changed Jacob's name to *Israel* . . .

## Jacob's Name Change

<u>Gen 32:28</u> – *Jacob To Israel*

> 28 AND HE SAID, **THY NAME SHALL BE CALLED NO MORE JACOB, BUT ISRAEL**: FOR AS A PRINCE HAST THOU POWER WITH GOD AND WITH MEN, AND HAST PREVAILED. **KJV**

because Jacob overcame the fears of his Old Man. After that, Righteous Adam, Jacob's New Man, who has the nature of God, prevailed over Esau.

<u>Col 3:9-10</u> – *The New Man*

> 9 LIE NOT ONE TO ANOTHER, SEEING THAT YE HAVE PUT OFF **THE OLD MAN** WITH HIS DEEDS;

> 10 AND HAVE PUT ON **THE NEW MAN**, WHICH IS RENEWED IN KNOWLEDGE AFTER THE IMAGE OF HIM THAT CREATED HIM: **KJV**

## Jacob Prevails

What did Righteous Adam mean when he said that Jacob prevailed with God and men?

First of all, the word *men*, really should say, *man*, because the word signifies *fallen Adam.*

Mortal man has an evil side. It is the mind of fallen Adam. Paul calls it *the carnal mind*, or *the mind of the flesh*

The correct understanding (despite the incorrect translation in the Scripture), is that Jacob took the victory over his fear of Esau when he submitted to Adam, his righteous side . . .

> **Gen 32:26** – *Adam Breaks Forth*
>
> 26 AND HE SAID, LET ME GO, *FOR THE DAY BREAKETH.* AND HE SAID, I WILL NOT LET THEE GO, EXCEPT THOU BLESS ME. **KJV**

and then Righteous Adam rose above Jacob's carnal mind and defeated Esau in a spiritual battle.

Jacob prevailed over his own carnal mind *because* of Righteous Adam, God's strength.

After that, Jacob, through Righteous Adam, the strength of God within himself, prevailed over the carnal mind of the man, Esau.

And that is how Jacob *prevailed over the fears of his own human nature, and over the man, Esau, because of his relationship with God*, through his inner man, called *Righteous Adam* in the Old Testament and *Christ Jesus* in the New Testament.

# V.

# SPIRITUAL DECEPTION

# V.
# SPIRITUAL DECEPTION

# ISAAC

## Jehovah's Female Power, Her Seed & The Shekinah

It is true that Jacob deceived Isaac, but it was necessary, because Isaac, himself, was deceived.

Jehovah's female power, together with her seed in Jacob, which was attached to him in the form of an Angel . . .

> **Gen 48:16** – *Angel Which Redeemed Me*
>
> 16 THE ANGEL WHICH REDEEMED ME FROM ALL EVIL, BLESS THE LADS; AND LET MY NAME BE NAMED ON THEM, AND THE NAME OF MY FATHERS ABRAHAM AND ISAAC; AND LET THEM GROW INTO A MULTITUDE IN THE MIDST OF THE EARTH. **KJV**

or an inner man, is called, *the Shekinah*.

Jehovah's female power, can be called *the Shekinah* only when she and her seed are in agreement. The unified singularity of *Mother and Daughter* in a man, is called *the Shekinah*.

The seed of Jehovah's female power, the Daughter, is grafted to the mam and eventually becomes the mortal man's Righteous Side.

> **James 1:8** – *Double minded Man*
>
> 8 A **DOUBLE MINDED MAN** IS UNSTABLE IN ALL HIS WAYS.
> **KJV**

Sometimes the carnal mind of the man overcomes his Righteous Side, to prevent him from agreeing with Jehovah's female power. In that event, *the Shekinah*, the power of God, does not materialize, and we see only *Jehovah's female power, the Spiritual Mother*.

# The Spiritual Inheritance

The Patriarchs had the ability to impart spiritual power to their children, so the issue between Esau and Jacob was not merely a blessing. *The issue was the transference of the promised seed to the son who would follow Jehovah's instructions, and the impartation of the power to bring it to fruition in mankind. The fate of the whole world hung in the balance.*

Isaac was dying and the inheritance urgently needed to be transferred to Jacob, the son that Jehovah elected to carry the accoutrements of salvation to the next generation.

> **Rom 9:10-12** – *Jacob Elected*
>
> 10 AND NOT ONLY THIS; BUT WHEN REBECCA ALSO HAD CONCEIVED BY ONE, EVEN BY OUR FATHER ISAAC;
>
> 11 (FOR THE CHILDREN BEING NOT YET BORN, NEITHER HAVING DONE ANY GOOD OR EVIL, THAT **THE PURPOSE OF GOD ACCORDING TO ELECTION** MIGHT STAND, NOT OF WORKS, BUT OF HIM THAT CALLETH;)
>
> 12 IT WAS SAID UNTO HER, **THE ELDER SHALL SERVE**

THE YOUNGER. **KJV**

# Disciples of The Shekinah

Isaac was bound under the authority of *the Shekinah*,[12] who met all of his needs, but he had no spiritual power of his own. In the following generation, *the Shekinah* extended her spiritual provision to mankind though the microcosm of Esau and Jacob: Esau inherited spiritual power that can be likened to the outpouring of the Holy Spirit, and Jacob inherited his father's personal relationship with the Shekinah, without any spiritual power.

Isaac's unfulfilled desire for spiritual power made him vulnerable to the seductive nature of the female spiritual power that Esau was wielding. He mistakenly believed that it was superior to the less dramatic and all but invisible benefits of the discipleship that he, as well as Jacob, were receiving from *the Shekinah*, their spiritual Mother.

Isaac was influenced by Esau's strong personality and mind control. Isaac ran after Esau because he thought that Esau's female spirituality proved that he was the true heir, but Isaac was mistaken. Surely the Lord must have told Isaac that the Inheritance was going to the wrong son *before* he sent Jacob to stop him from making a disastrous mistake. But Isaac did not hear the warnings.

In addition to Isaac's misunderstanding of Jehovah Plan of Salvation, Isaac thought that Esau, his eldest son, his first born, should inherit all of his spiritual and worldly possessions, in accordance with the Natural Law of Primogeniture.

---

[12] See, ***Christ-Centered Kabbalah*** Message #661, ***Isaac, A Well of Living Waters***, a study in the ***Soncino Zohar***, Bereshith, Section 1, Page 135b

The Scripture says that Jacob's mother, Rebecca, deviously devised the scheme to deceive Isaac. In fact, the letter of the Word makes both Rebecca and Jacob look pretty ungodly! But to those who believe the Spirit of the Word, Jehovah sent *the Shekinah*, *Jacob's spiritual Mother*, to instruct him about his part in preserving the promised seed the source of salvation for all mankind.

**Gal 3:29** – *Abraham's Seed*

> 29 AND IF YE BE CHRIST'S, THEN ARE YE ABRAHAM'S SEED, AND HEIRS ACCORDING TO THE PROMISE. **KJV**

The story turns out the same, either way: The seed is safely passed to Jacob, and from there to Judah, Joseph and Jesus. Jacob knew that he, and not Esau, was supposed to inherit the seed, so, for him it was like taking what already belonged to him. Isaac and Esau were not hearing from God, so they did not understand that Jehovah had rejected Esau and chose Jacob in his place.

In any event, Esau took heathen wives, so the promised seed would have been corrupted if Esau had inherited it.

# A Lesson Learned

There is a powerful lesson here. Spiritual gifts and spiritual power are not qualifying signs of leadership, or authority. A spiritually powerful person, someone who receives words of knowledge, for example, is not necessarily ready to exercise spiritual authority, or assist those who exercise authority. Spirituality, speaking in tongues, prophesying, and other gifts, do not indicate preparedness for ministry. The signs of preparedness are, stability and commitment, keeping your word, laboring faithfully, and the ability and willingness to submit to authority.

# Esau's Hairy Skin

Was *Esau* so hairy, that his skin was likened to a goat's skin?

### Gen 27:11 – *A Hairy Man*

> 11 AND JACOB SAID TO REBEKAH HIS MOTHER, BEHOLD, ESAU **MY BROTHER IS A HAIRY MAN**, AND I AM A SMOOTH MAN: **KJV**

It is more likely that Esau was spiritually hairy, like Elijah. That is, Esau had so much spiritual energy that it flowed out from his inward parts and surrounded him on the outside.

Kabbalah calls spiritual light, either *inner light,* or *surrounding light*.

Practitioners of New Age spirituality call surrounding light, *aura*.

Peter seems to have had an abundance of surrounding light also. The New Testament calls it *his shadow*. Whoever Peter's shadow passed over was healed of their diseases.

### Acts 5:15 – *Peter's Shadow*

> 15 INSOMUCH THAT THEY BROUGHT FORTH THE SICK INTO THE STREETS, AND LAID THEM ON BEDS AND COUCHES, THAT AT THE LEAST **THE SHADOW OF PETER PASSING BY MIGHT OVERSHADOW SOME OF THEM. KJV**

# JACOB

## Jacob's Integrity

Everyone with spiritual eyes could see that Jacob was a man of God. Jacob's carnal mind was bound under his God mind so securely that, for all intents and purpose, he had only one mind, *the Righteous mind of God*. But Jacob lacked spiritual power,

## Jacob's Weakness

How could Jacob, one of the fathers of Israel, be such a morally weak man that he would steal his brother's blessing?

The answer is that Jehovah told Jacob to do all that he did. The Scripture says that Rebecca instructed Jacob, but it is more likely that it was Ima, the partsuf of Binah of the World of Emanation called, *Mother*, that advised him.

Ima spoke to Jacob through his own mind. The conflict that the Scripture records is actually between Jacob's human side, his carnal mind, and Ima.

> 11 MY FATHER PERADVENTURE WILL FEEL ME, AND I SHALL SEEM TO HIM AS A DECEIVER; **AND I SHALL BRING A CURSE UPON ME**, AND NOT A BLESSING.

> 12 AND HIS MOTHER SAID UNTO HIM, **UPON ME BE THY CURSE, MY SON: ONLY OBEY MY VOICE**, AND GO FETCH ME THEM.  **KJV**

# SPIRITUAL POWER

## Hands

Hands signify the two minds, the human (carnal) mind, and the God (Christ) mind.

Did *Jacob* really put goat skins on the back of his neck and on his hands?

Gen 27:16

16 And **she put the skins of the kids of the goats upon his hands**, and upon the smooth of his neck: KJV

## Jacob's Hand

Spiritually speaking, the mind is like a hand, because the mind grasps. It grasps ideas. It also grasps people's souls. The mind is a spiritual hand, so we can spiritually feel after someone with our mind. This experience is called *discernment*.

<u>Gen 27:21</u> – *Isaac's Discernment*

21 AND ISAAC SAID UNTO JACOB, **COME NEAR, I PRAY THEE, THAT I MAY FEEL THEE**, MY SON, WHETHER THOU BE MY VERY SON ESAU OR NOT. **KJV**

Isaac wanted to confirm Jacob's identity with discernment, so he asked to *feel* him. Isaac's request had nothing to do with touching Jacob's hands or neck to see how physically hairy he was.

### Acts 17:27 – *Feeling With Your mind*

> 27 THAT THEY SHOULD SEEK THE LORD, IF
> **HAPLY THEY MIGHT FEEL AFTER HIM, AND FIND HIM,**
> THOUGH HE BE NOT FAR FROM EVERY ONE OF US: **KJV**

Isaac relied on his own ability to spiritually discern the identity of his son. He did not seek the counsel of the Shekinah, his spiritual mother. In short, Isaac followed after the spiritual gifts, rather than the wisdom of God.

# Neck

The neck signifies the fifth energy center. The Jews call it *the neck*, but Hindus and New Agers call it *the throat center*.

*The function of the throat center is the exercise of spiritual power through the spoken word.*

There is only one fifth energy center, but there are two doors, so to speak, by which it can be accessed: The neck and the throat, or, we can say, the front door and the back door.

Jew, Hindu and New Ager, alike, access the fifth energy center. The only difference is the motive of the person accessing the center, and the mind that they use to access it.

The mind of God uses the front door, which is the neck . . .

### Song 4:4 – *An Ivory Neck*

> 4 THY NECK IS LIKE THE TOWER OF DAVID
> BUILDED FOR AN ARMOURY, WHEREON THERE HANG A
> THOUSAND BUCKLERS, ALL SHIELDS OF MIGHTY MEN. **KJV**

but the carnal mind uses the back door, which is the throat.

The throat always signifies evil . . .

### Ps 5:9 – *The Throat*

> 9 FOR THERE IS NO FAITHFULNESS IN THEIR MOUTH; THEIR INWARD PART IS VERY WICKEDNESS; **THEIR THROAT IS AN OPEN SEPULCHRE**; THEY FLATTER WITH THEIR TONGUE. **KJV**

# Spoken Spiritual Power

Some justify the use of spiritual power based upon their own subjective morality. They believe it is okay if it is for a good purpose, such as physical or emotional healing, or to break a curse, but this is not true. The wielding of spiritual power based upon the moral judgment of a mortal man calls forth the same unhappy consequences, whether it is done for evil, or for what appears to be a good motive.

Only God can make the moral judgment about when to use spiritual power.

### John 11:43 – *Lazarus, Come Forth*

> 43 AND WHEN HE THUS HAD SPOKEN, **HE CRIED WITH A LOUD VOICE, LAZARUS, COME FORTH. KJV**

Spiritual power spoken through the mind of God is permitted, but the illegal use of the powers of the throat energy center is called *sorcery*, which is strictly forbidden.

## *Ivory* and Spiritual Power

*Ivory* in Scripture signifies the spoken spiritual power of the neck energy center.

### Song 7:4 – *Tower of Ivory*

> 4 THY NECK IS AS A TOWER OF IVORY; THINE EYES LIKE THE FISHPOOLS IN HESHBON, BY THE GATE OF BATH-RABBIM: THY NOSE IS AS THE TOWER OF LEBANON WHICH LOOKETH TOWARD DAMASCUS. **KJV**

Solomon wielded a high degree of Jehovah's spiritual power before he turned away from the one true God to idols, and Solomon had an ivory throne.

### 1 Kings 10:18 – *Throne of Ivory*

> 18 MOREOVER THE KING MADE **A GREAT THRONE OF IVORY**, AND OVERLAID IT WITH THE BEST GOLD. **KJV**

## The Power of Illusion

Rebecca sacrificed the two kids to Jehovah . . .

### Gen 27:9 – *Jacob's Sacrifice*

> 9 GO NOW TO THE FLOCK, AND FETCH ME FROM **THENCE TWO GOOD KIDS OF THE GOATS**; AND I WILL MAKE THEM SAVOURY MEAT FOR THY FATHER, SUCH AS HE LOVETH: **KJV**

and Jehovah granted Rebekah the spiritual power of illusion.

Hair signifies the animal spirituality. Rebekah covered the energy of Jacob's Righteous mind with the illusion of Esau's animal (carnal) mind, and she made the energy of Jacob's neck center appear to be the energy of his throat (the back of his neck), which emanates from the animal nature.

# ISAAC

## Isaac's Blessing

*Isaac's blessing* was a religious ritual that passed Jehovah's promises to Abraham and Isaac on to the next generation. It also released spiritual power and authority to the recipient.

*Isaac's blessing* was a religious ritual energized by an animal sacrifice. Spilling the blood of the animal released a third-party energy, so to speak, that attached itself to the promised seed within Isaac when he ate the animal's flesh. That energy, with the promised seed attached, then returned to Jacob, the one who slaughtered the animal, when Jacob kissed him.

### Gen 27:26-27 - *The Kiss*

26 AND HIS FATHER ISAAC SAID UNTO HIM, COME NEAR NOW, **AND KISS ME, MY SON.**

27 AND HE CAME NEAR, AND KISSED HIM: KJV

The ritual was like a boomerang: The energy released from the slaughtered animal, took up residence in the hunter.

### Gen 27:3-4 – *Meat For Isaac*

3 NOW THEREFORE *TAKE*, I PRAY THEE, **THY WEAPONS, THY QUIVER AND THY BOW, AND GO OUT TO THE FIELD, AND TAKE ME SOME VENISON;**

4 **AND MAKE ME SAVOURY MEAT,** SUCH AS I LOVE, AND BRING IT TO ME, THAT I MAY EAT; THAT MY

SOUL MAY BLESS THEE BEFORE I DIE. **KJV**

Isaac knew that it was Jacob and not Esau because he recognized Jacob's voice . . .

### Gen 27:22-23 – *Discerned Him Not*

22 AND JACOB WENT NEAR UNTO ISAAC HIS FATHER; AND HE FELT HIM, AND SAID, **THE VOICE IS JACOB'S VOICE, BUT THE HANDS ARE THE HANDS OF ESAU.**

23 **AND HE DISCERNED HIM NOT, BECAUSE HIS HANDS WERE HAIRY,** AS HIS BROTHER ESAU'S HANDS: SO HE BLESSED HIM. **KJV**

and Isaac should have been able to tell the difference between the venison that he requested of Esau, and the goat's meat that Jacob brought him.

But Isaac responded to the spirit of the animal nature that emanated from Jacob because of Rebecca's illusion, even though his own ears and mind told him that his visitor was Jacob and not Esau. But, more importantly, Isaac did not ask the Shekinah, who was building the male spirituality in him, to help him discern the truth.

## Male and Female Spirituality

Isaac had an ungodly soul tie with Esau based upon the emotionalism of the female spirituality.

The male spirituality develops a base of spiritual wisdom and esoteric doctrine out of which a stream of controlled spiritual power eventually bursts forth, to restrain and weaken the animal nature.

The male spirituality is the mind of God.

The female spirituality is raw spiritual power that lacks wisdom. The Holy Spirit is not controlled by a mind. It diffuses in all directions until it dissipates

We live by the wisdom of God, not by the female spirituality, which may or may not be of God, because Satan, the unconscious part of the carnal mind, counterfeits the Holy Spirit.

**1 Cor 11:14** – *Satan Transformed*

> 14 AND NO MARVEL; FOR SATAN HIMSELF IS TRANSFORMED INTO AN ANGEL OF LIGHT. **KJV**

Dreams, revelations, prophecy and discernment are spiritual gifts that operate out of the female spirituality of the natural man. We cannot live by these alone. Christ Jesus, the wisdom of God within us, must have the last word on everything that we do. We escape the destruction that is in this world through the lust of the natural man to control the circumstances of his life, by living out of the Christ mind.

# Esau's Birthright

This is why Esau sold his birthright. . . .

**Gen 25:30-31** – *Sell Me Thy Birthright*

> 30 AND ESAU SAID TO JACOB, **FEED ME, I PRAY THEE, WITH THAT SAME RED POTTAGE; FOR I AM FAINT:** THEREFORE WAS HIS NAME CALLED EDOM.

> 31 AND JACOB SAID, **SELL ME THIS DAY THY BIRTHRIGHT.** **KJV**

Esau's spirit was depleted, and esoteric doctrine, alone,

replenishes the Spirit. Jacob studied Kabbalah, but Esau despised study and the exposure of sin that results from it. Esau was the brother with the branch of the tree. He had all of the spiritual energy, but he was not responsible or emotionally or intellectually stable. Jacob had the root of the tree. He was faithful and stable, but he had no power. Esau sold his birthright in exchange for the temporary satisfaction of a spiritual need that he could have satisfied himself.

The Scripture does not say these things clearly. What it does say is, *he who has ears to hear, let him hear*, and to the others, *let them go in peace*.

# Reaping What You Sow

Jacob had to use a method of this world to acquire a blessing that God said was his, because he had not yet attained to the degree of spiritual maturity by which he could have accomplished his goal without sin.

It is wrong to deceive your father and steal from your brother. Jacob sinned and reaped what he sowed, even though he did what the Shekinah told him to do.

Jacob had to leave his home and his family after Esau threatened to kill him. After that, he was afflicted and robbed by Laban his father-in-law for fourteen years.

Jacob stole, and Laban stole from Jacob. Jacob dishonored his father, and faced the possibility of an untimely death at the hands of Esau, his brother.

Jacob feared Esau because he knew that he had violated the Fifth Commandment, . . .

**Ex 20:12** – *Honour Thy Father & Mother*

12 HONOUR THY FATHER AND THY MOTHER: THAT THY DAYS MAY BE LONG UPON THE LAND WHICH THE LORD THY GOD GIVETH THEE. KJV

wherefore it was very possible that Esau might murder him and his whole family. But God intervened to save Jacob from destruction because Jacob had fulfilled God's will, even though he had done it imperfectly.

# Another Testimony

This very same spiritual principal manifested in my own life.

I live in a condominium. The Lord raised me up to unseat the woman who was president, because she was abusing her office. She was stealing from the condominium. I was the vessel that God used to unseat her. Then I became president, and then I reaped what I had sown.

The same thing that I had done to unseat the previous president, was happening to me. The Board of Managers that I presided over rebelled against me. I could not understand why I would have the same experience, since I was serving God by doing what I did.

The Lord explained it to me this way: I did not have the spiritual power or authority to unseat the previous president strictly with spiritual power. I had to do things in the natural that are not acceptable to God. I had to rebel against the established authority, for example, to unseat her. Therefore, when I became president, my board rebelled against me. I had to reap what I sowed even though I was fulfilling God's purposes, because I fulfilled those purposes imperfectly.

The Lord will always stop the sowing and reaping judgment short of destruction when you are reaping judgment because of your imperfect service to him. I had to reap what I sowed, and Jacob had to reap what he sowed. But Jacob is still reaping today, every time some Bible believer calls him a deceiver or a thief.

I will not call Jacob a deceiver. I know what he did was deception, but he did it to serve God and to save the promised seed. If Isaac had passed that holy seed to Esau, it would have been corrupted by Esau's heathen wives, and Jehovah's plan to save the world would have been destroyed. He would have had to find another Abraham and start all over.

# VI.

# THE EURO-PALESTINE - ISRAEL CONFLICT

# VI.
# THE EURO-PALESTINE - ISRAEL CONFLICT

# THE ISSUE OF KHAZARIA

## Israel's Right to The Land

### *The Palestinian Position*

The Palestinians and their supporters in Europe and the United States say that the Jewish people, of which I am one, are not the Jews of the Bible. They say that we are not the physical descendants of Abraham, Isaac and Jacob, but are the descendants of a medieval East European nation that converted to Judaism, called *Khazaria*. They say, further, that Israel does not belong in the Middle East because the people of Israel are not Middle Eastern or Semitic. They are European descendants of Japheth.

### *The Questions*

Is the modern-day Jew the Semitic Jew of the Bible, the physical descendants of Abraham, Isaac and Jacob?

Are they the very same Jewish people who were scattered all over the world after Herod's temple was destroyed?

Or are their forefathers Khazarians, medieval East European

converts to Judaism, the descendants of Japheth?

An Internet search for the terms *Khazar, Khazarian*, etc. turns up a slew of anti-Semitic articles and websites which usually deny the holocaust, as well as Israel's right to exist.

## The Search for The Truth

My initial reaction to the issue of the *Khazarian Jews* was, *how utterly ridiculous,* but the idea stayed with me, and, eventually, I learned that someone had written a book on the subject, called *The Thirteenth Tribe*. (Arthur Koestler, Random House, NY, 1975).

I was taught to always listen and seriously consider both sides of an issue, so I knew that I had to read that book before I could refute *that ridiculous argument* intelligently. Besides, I thought, surely, the author must be a non-Jew and an anti- Semite.

To my absolute amazement, I found *The Thirteenth Tribe* to be a very scholarly book. Arthur Koestler, the author of *The Thirteenth Tribe*, is a Jewish anthropologist who is associated with one of the most respected universities in Modern-Day Israel. He is a scholar who seriously believes, on good evidence, that the Jews of today are not the Jews of Bible days, the physical descendants of Jacob, and he makes a very good case for his theory. I could not perceive any prejudice in the book, and must admit that there was no reason whatsoever to believe that Mr. Koestler is an anti-Semite!

Mr. Koestler claims that there was a small, heretofore insignificant European nation, called, *Khazaria,* that existed in medieval times. The King of Khazaria and his subjects converted to Judaism, which then became the national religion of Khazaria. Freedom of religion for those who preferred another faith was, however, permitted.

Mr. Koestler describes Khazaria, based upon his anthropological findings, as an ***insignificant, small heretofore unknown European nation of white people***.

According to Mr. Koestler, the entire Khazarian Empire were introduced to Judaism, embraced it as it is laid out in the Torah and other books, and are the ancestors of the people who are known today as ***the Jewish people***.

Mr. Koestler's conclusions agree with those of Simon Dubow, ***History of the Jews in Russia and Poland from the Earliest Times Until the Present Day*** (Simom Dubnow, www.Forgtten Books.com, 2. Vol 1, Chap I, THE DIASPORA IN EASTERN EUROPE, 2. The Kingdom of the Khazars, pp 19-28).

Mr. Dubow says on page 20:

> THE CONVERSION OF THE KHAZARS TO JUDAISM, WHICH TOOK PLACE ABOUT 740, IS DESCRIBED CIRCUMSTANTIALLY IN THE TRADITIONS PRESERVED AMONG THE JEWS ...

# Israelite or Khazarian?

All of my life, I have been told that the Jewish people are a Semitic people, the offspring of Shem. But I do not look like a Semite. I am a very pale-skinned person. My heritage is Hungarian, and I look Hungarian. I know a lot of Jews who come from Russia, and they look Russian. They are very white.

I could never understand how a Semitic, dark-skinned people that emigrated from the Middle East to Europe, would take on the physical characteristics of those nations. How could they become white and look like the citizens of their host nation, apart from intermarriage? I have been aware of this contradiction for a long time, and never did understand it.

## Preamble To The Conclusion

*Conversion* means that the God of the religion that you convert to joins himself to you. In the case of Judaism, it also means that the convert receives a Jewish soul.

So, if it is true, that the modern Jew, of which I am one, is not a physical descendant of Abraham, Isaac and Jacob, the Jew of the Bible; if we are a different nation than the Jew of the Bible, there is, nevertheless, historical evidence that we are legitimate converts to Judaism, and, if converts, then true Jews.

The incredible amount of knowledge and wisdom that the modern-day Jews have preserved and made available to the world are further indications that Spiritual Israel are incarnate in them.

## Conclusion

MY RESPONSE TO ALL THE HOLOCAUST-DENYING VOICES THAT CLAIM THAT THE ASHKENAZI JEWS HAVE NO RIGHT TO THE LAND OF ISRAEL, IS THIS:

THE MODERN-DAY JEW, THE PHYSICAL DESCENDANTS OF ABRAHAM, ISAAC AND JACOB, AS WELL AS ALL CONVERTS, HAVE A LEGITIMATE RIGHT TO THE PROMISES THAT JEHOVAH MADE TO ABRAHAM, ISAAC AND JACOB, INCLUDING THE RIGHT TO THE LAND OF ISRAEL, ACCORDING TO THE BORDERS DESCRIBED IN THE TORAH.

# TABLE OF REFERENCES

# ABOUT THE AUTHOR

Sheila R. Vitale is the Spiritual Leader, Founding Teacher, and Pastor of *Living Epistles Ministries (LEM)*. She moves in the offices of Teacher of Apostolic Doctrine, Prophet, Evangelist and Pastor, has an international following, and has been expounding on the Scripture through a unique spiritual lens for nearly three decades.

She has written more than 50 books based on the Old and New Testaments including *Ephraim, Man of the Earth* and *The Eagle Ascended (OT),* and *Salvation* and *Not Without Blood (NT).* She has also rendered original spiritual interpretations of Biblical texts such as *The Woman in The Well (John, Chapter 4)* and *First Corinthians, Chapter 11.* Her unique, Multi-Part Message style is seen in *LEM* Serial Messages such as *A Place Teeming With Life* (9 Parts) and *Quantum Mechanics in Creation* (18 Parts). Each Part of a Multi-Part Message Series can also be enjoyed as a complete and independent study. In addition, she has defined, explained, illustrated and demonstrated hundreds of spiritual principles throughout more than 1,000 *LEM* Lectures.

Her signature work, however, is the three volumes of *The Alternate Translation Bible (ATB)*: *The Alternate Translation of The Old Testament*, *The Alternate Translation of The New Testament* and *The Alternate Translation of the Book of Revelation. The Alternate Translation Bible* is a work in progress (*The ATB Project*). Accordingly, additional spiritual interpretations of both whole and partial Chapters are added from time to time, as they are rendered. The most up-to-date versions of *The ATB Project* may be found online at *The LEM* W*ebsite* (*LivingEpistles.org*). *The ATB* is a *spiritual interpretation* of the Scripture and is not intended to replace traditional translations.

She also analyzed the Greek text of *The Book of Revelation* and preached extensively on it in the early years of *The ATB Project*. During that time she produced 197 distinct *Message*

*Parts*, under 29 specific *Message Titles*, all of which deal with *The Book of Revelation*. Also, many of her books such as, *Adam and The Two Judgments* and *A Study in Unconscious Mind Control*, have been translated into Spanish, as well as *The Book of Revelation*.

Pastor Vitale is an illustrator of spiritual principles, a researcher, a translator and a reviewer of the Modern Social Trends of Family and Culture, as they are revealed through TV programs (*The Sopranos),* movies (*The Matrix* and *The Edge of Tomorrow)* and plays (*Wicked)*. She also writes for the *LEM Blog*.

She travels domestically, as well as internationally, preaching and teaching Judeo-Christian Spiritual Philosophy, and has donated Audio Libraries of her Lectures to other ministries in Africa, Asia, Europe and North America,

Pastor Vitale serves *LEM* in a range of spiritual, educational, and administrative functions from *The Selden Centre*, *LEM* headquarters in Selden, New York. She is also a philanthropic individual who supports the *Lighthouse Mission (Patchogue, NY) and HGM – Mission of Hope – Haiti, and other* charitable organizations. She also supports community services such as the *Terryville Fire Department*.

In her spare time, Pastor Vitale enjoys watching movies, attending plays and partaking of cuisines from different cultures. An avid traveler, she has visited several countries in Europe and Africa as well as many cities in the United States.

# BEGINNINGS, INSPIRATION AND CALLING

Pastor Vitale began her spiritual journey as a child when her Jewish mother enrolled her in the Hebrew school of an

Orthodox synagogue. She experienced the Spirit of God for the first time there in such a profound way that she wept. But after that, when she was only eleven years old, she became very ill and was taken to Mount Sinai Hospital in New York City. She almost died there and has battled with life-threatening health issues ever since. Nevertheless, a deep longing for God continued to pursue her until several years later when she desperately wanted to attend Yeshiva (Jewish high school), but could not. Her secular parents approved of her choice, but could not afford the tuition.

Much later, after years of searching, she once again experienced the Spirit that had brought her to tears in the synagogue of her youth, but this time it was at *Gospel Revivals Ministries*, a Pentecostal church where Deliverance Ministry was emphasized. She had a desire to understand the Bible since she was a child, but Scripture was difficult for her and she struggled with the text. Nevertheless, she read one Chapter of the Bible every day until, one day, *her spiritual eyes opened* and she saw an angel holding a little book.

After that, she attended as many as five teaching services each week for about seven years, the latter part of which she edited *Pastor Holzhauser's* books. But several more years had to pass before *the eyes of her understanding opened even further* and she began to receive *Revelation Knowledge of the Scripture*. She understood at that time that the angel she had seen was the angel of Revelation 10:8.

After about seven years of learning *Deliverance Ministry* and *The Doctrine of Sonship (Bill Britton)* from *Pastor Holzhauser,* she studied the Bible independently under the influence and direction of the Holy Spirit.

In **1998** she began teaching Apostolic Doctrine.

In **1990** she spent three months in Stony Brook Hospital where she recovered from an incurable disease, defeating premature death, once again, and went on to resume teaching and managing *LEM*.

In **1992** she journeyed to Africa for the first time, where she was called to the office of Evangelist.

In the **mid-1990s,** she began to Pastor in addition to being a Teacher of Apostolic Doctrine, a Prophet and an Evangelist, thus, satisfying all five offices of *The Ministry of the Lord Jesus Christ to His Church.*

# LIVING EPISTLES MINISTRIES

Pastor Vitale was happy fellowshipping at *Gospel Revivals Ministries* but, eventually, she desired a deeper and more spiritual understanding of the Word of God. One day, after crying out to Jesus about her need, she was amazed to hear Him ask her if she would teach. Her initial response was that she did not see how it would be possible since she was already working a full-time job, despite her poor health. But after the Lord asked her for a second and then a third time, she reluctantly agreed, believing that He would empower her to do the job. Shortly thereafter, in the latter part of 1987, she began to teach her own brand of Judeo-Christian Spiritual Philosophy.

The Lord Jesus Christ named the work *Living Epistles Ministries* in 1988.

The first *LEM* meetings were casual and spontaneous gatherings of friends and fellow deliverance workers in Pastor Vitale's home. After that, they were held in the business office of one of the brethren. Pastor Vitale delivered her first formal message entitled *The Truth About Witchcraft in January of 1988,* followed by *The Seduction of Eve* in April of the same year. After that, she prepared and taught weekly messages including *Signs of Apostleship* and *Lazarus & The Rich Man.* The meetings eventually increased to two and then three each week.

Sometime after that, she learned that the Lord Jesus Christ

was revealing spiritual principles from the Hebrew text of the Old Testament through her teachings, and she used those spiritual principles to begin to unlock the mysteries of the New Testament, as well. Today she understands that the Scripture is a spiritual document that must be spiritually discerned if it is to be understood correctly, and calls that spiritual understanding **The Doctrine of Christ**.

*LEM* publishes a wide range of material, including books, e-books, spiritual interpretations of the Scripture and transcripts of many of Pastor Vitale's Lectures and on-line meetings, all of which, as well as the entire *Alternate Translation Bible,* may be viewed free of charge on the *LEM* website (*LivingEpistles.org*). She also has an *Author's Website* where all of her books, as well as several photographs of herself and a short biography are displayed (Amazon.com/author/SheilaVitale). Paperback and digital versions of *LEM* books may be purchased through *Amazon, Google Books* and *Barnes & Noble.*

*LEM* provides free video livestreams through YouTube and other Internet Platforms . . .

> *@LivingEpistlesMinistries* ( 2016 – Sept. 2022)
> *@LivingEpistlesMinistriesLEM* ((Oct. 2022 – Ongoing)
> *@LivingEpistlesMinistries* (LEM disciples)

. . . as well as two channels of **Shortclips** where short, focused messages of about 15 minutes each are posted:

> *@shortclipsbysheilar.vitale3334* (2016 – Sept. 2022)
> *@ShortClips-SheilaVitale* (Oct. 2022 – Ongoing)

*LEM* donates a significant percentage of its income to other Christian ministries and organizations that advocate for Christian values and defend the United States Constitution.

# PASTOR VITALE TODAY

Today Pastor Vitale continues to dedicate her life to teaching the spiritual principles of the Bible and focuses daily on studying, writing and preaching powerful messages from *The Selden Centre,* LEM/CCK's headquarters at Selden, New York.

# The Three Israels

**Including:**

The Mystery of Black Israel

The Spiritual Roots of the Jewish People

The Spiritual Roots of the Euro-Palestine – Israel Conflict

The Issue of Khazaria

Sheila R. Vitale

Christ-Centered Kabbalah

# Living Epistles Ministries
## Sheila R. Vitale
Pastor, Teacher & Founder
Judeo-Christian Spiritual Philosophy
PO Box 562, Port Jefferson Station, New York 11776, USA
LivingEpistles.org
*or*
Books@LivingEpistles.org